MYTHS AND LIES ABOUT DADS

Myths and Lies About Dads: How They Hurt Us All is a groundbreaking book that destroys more than 100 of the most damaging beliefs about fathers. Using the most recent research, this pioneering work exposes these baseless beliefs and the toll they take on children's relationships with their fathers, parents' relationships with one another, and the physical and mental health of fathers and mothers. Tackling a wide range of topics from custody laws, to children's toys, to the sexist behavior of counselors, pediatricians, and lawyers, Dr Linda Nielsen describes in vivid detail how these myths are linked to many of our most pressing issues:

- Creating more gender equity in childcare and housework
- Reducing child abuse, post-partum depression, and fathers' suicide rates
- Expanding mothers' and fathers' options at home and at work
- Reducing children's academic, behavioral, and emotional problems
- Lessening the pressures of parenting for both parents
- Changing sexist policies and practices that hurt parents and children
- Improving the economic situations for parents and their children

The book is not only a wake-up call for parents but also for students and professionals in medicine and family law, social work, child development, education, and in the publishing, advertising, media, and entertainment industries. Above all, the book empowers parents to free themselves from the myths and lies about fathers that bind them.

Dr Linda Nielsen is a Professor of Education at Wake Forest University in Winston-Salem, NC. An international authority on father-daughter relationships and shared parenting for separated parents, her work has been featured in a PBS documentary and in the media, including the BBC, NPR, *New York Times*, *Wall Street Journal*, *Washington Post*, *Time*, and *Oprah*.

T0383531

Linda Nielsen is a Professor of Adolescent and Educational Psychology at Wake Forest University (US). A member of the faculty for 35 years, she is a nationally recognized expert on father-daughter relationships.

Also by Linda Nielsen

Improving Father-Daughter Relationships: A Guide for Women & Their Dads
ISBN 9780367524272

This friendly, no-nonsense book offers women and their dads a step-by-step guide to improve their relationships and to understand the impact this will have on their well-being. Nielsen encourages us to get to the root of problems, instead of dealing with fallout, and helps us resolve the conflicts that commonly strain relationships from late adolescence throughout a daughter's adult year.

Father-Daughter Relationships: Contemporary Research and Issues Second edition
ISBN 9780367232870

This essential text summarizes and analyses the most relevant research regarding father-daughter relationships, aiming to break down the persistent misconceptions regarding fatherhood and father-daughter relationships and encourage the reader to take a more objective and analytical approach.

MYTHS AND LIES ABOUT DADS

HOW THEY HURT US ALL

Linda Nielsen

Routledge
Taylor & Francis Group

NEW YORK AND LONDON

Cover image: *Awakenings* by Steve Mizel at Mizelart.com

First published 2023
by Routledge
605 Third Avenue, New York, NY 10158

and by Routledge
4 Park Square, Milton Park, Abingdon, Oxon, OX14 4RN

Routledge is an imprint of the Taylor & Francis Group, an informa business

ISBN: 9781032348254 (hbk)
ISBN: 9781032348230 (pbk)
ISBN: 9781003324003 (ebk)

DOI: 10.4324/9781003324003

Typeset in Bembo
by KnowledgeWorks Global Ltd.

To the fathers and students who shared and explored their experiences with me.

CONTENTS

ACKNOWLEDGMENTS

"There ain't nothing more to write about and I'm rotten glad of it, because if I'd know'd what trouble it was to make a book, I wouldn't a tackled it."
—*Mark Twain*

Unlike Mark Twain, I am glad I tackled this book. But for sure, Twain is still spot on when he complains that "making" a book is a lot of trouble. Perhaps now more than ever before, bringing any book to fruition depends on the work and dedication of many people. Indeed, even before I started writing this book, hundreds of other people were already involved in its creation. Chief among them are hundreds and hundreds of fathers and students who have shared their experiences with me and the dedicated researchers who produced the large body of research on which this book is founded.

I am indebted to the many fathers who have sought my advice and trusted me enough to share their personal fatherhood journeys and fathering experiences with me. I honor these men for their love and commitment to their sons and daughters, even in the most challenging, disheartening situations. I respect their resilience, openness, and willingness to explore ways to strengthen their bonds with their children—at whatever age. In that spirit, I value the work that organizations, such as City Dads Group, At Home Dads network, and National Parenting Organization, are doing on behalf of fathers—married dads, single dads, divorced dads, gay dads, very educated and not-so-educated dads, and dads of every age, race, and religion. In their own unique ways, these organizations are working to dispel the damaging myths and negative stereotypes that undermine fathers' relationships with their children and with the mothers of their children.

For more than three decades, my writing has also been informed and enriched by the male and female students in my "Fathers and Daughters" and "Children of Divorce" courses at Wake Forest University. These young adults inspire and motivate me as a teacher and as an author. They continue to impress and surprise me with their candor and their insight into their own families, especially their relationships with their dads. In humorous, heartfelt, and heartbreaking ways, they have taught me more than research data and statistics alone can capture. Some of their stories are included in this book with details and names changed to protect their privacy.

I am also grateful to several prominent experts whose pioneering work has had a profound impact on my teaching and writing over many years. For his work on fatherhood and male myths and stereotypes, I thank Dr. Warren Farrell. For her work on blended families and remarried fathers, I thank Dr. Patricia Papernow. For his work on alienated children and on shared parenting after divorce, I thank Dr. Richard Warshak whose insightful feedback has been invaluable to me over many years.

As members of the production team, many talented people at Routledge shepherded this book along the way. As senior editor, Helen Pitt has been an invaluable source of support and advice for all three of my books, finding a good home for them at Routledge. As senior project manager, Misbah Sabri has worked diligently and earnestly, paying careful attention to detail. And Martha Lentz of *Words Matter* greatly improved the clarity, flow, and organization of the book with her editorial suggestions and witty wording.

As I celebrate the completion of this book, I honor and embrace my closest friend who has given me his unrelenting, whole-hearted support for every book I have written—my loving husband, Steve Mizel. Not only does his beautiful art grace the covers of each of my books, he enriches my life beyond words—adding bold color as well as pastel nuances to each and every day.

Dr. Linda Nielsen
Professor of Education
Wake Forest University
Winston Salem, NC

FATHERS IN AMERICA

WHY WE BELIEVE WHAT ISN'T TRUE— AND WHY IT MATTERS

DOI: 10.4324/9781003324003-1

There are certain things we know for sure about American fathers, right? Most divorced dads do not pay any child support. Most married dads cheat, and in most divorces, the husband leaves his wife for a much younger woman. Most husbands are slouches on couches who don't do their fair share of the work in raising children. Mothers have an innate instinct for raising children that men lack. Newborns automatically form a strong emotional bond with their mothers, but not with their fathers. Men are not able to empathize or communicate with their children as well as women can.

There's only one problem here: Not one of these beliefs is true. If you thought they were, you are not alone. Many people, *including men,* believe these untrue things. Why? Because many of us have been duped, or have duped ourselves, into believing things about fathers that are completely untrue or are extreme exaggerations and distortions of the truth. We have bought into negative stereotypes about fathers that do not reflect reality. We have embraced many demeaning, insulting beliefs about fathers that are baseless and run counter to the research and to national statistics.

So what? Why get all riled up about negative stereotypes or baseless beliefs about fathers? Because, as researchers have been telling us for decades, our mistaken beliefs and unfounded stereotypes about any group of people have a negative impact on people's lives, as well as on our society's laws, policies, and practices. In the case of fathers, those stereotypes and baseless beliefs have an impact on millions of people—mainly on children but also on mothers and fathers. And that is what this book is about: identifying the father myths and stereotypes, exploring their damaging impact, and figuring out what to do about it.

WHY MYTHS AND STEREOTYPES MATTER

Let's take a closer look at stereotyping, leaving fathers aside for now. Focus on women. Now there's a stereotype rich topic. Since the 1960s when the feminist movement gained momentum, women have been fighting against sexist stereotypes and myths that demean, discourage, disenfranchise, and dismiss them. In waging this battle, women went after those who were sustaining and promoting those unfounded, exaggerated, or false beliefs, including the publishing, advertising, and film industries; public school and college books; toy companies, and even comedians. Why all the fuss about stereotypes? Because women realized something that researchers have documented for decades: Stereotypes and myths about any group of people play out in real life in ways that hurt and discriminate against people, sometimes for a lifetime.

Often the stereotypes and discrimination play out in such small, seemingly insignificant ways that we hardly notice them. Take, for example, the 1990s talking Barbie doll that got feminists so riled up because one of Barbie's phrases was "Math class is hard." Why the uproar? Because that little phrase reinforced the widespread stereotype that girls don't like math (or science), aren't very good at it, and "naturally" aren't interested in pursuing jobs in math or science. Given the ongoing barrage of "math is for boys" messages at the time, very few women were going into jobs in math or science—jobs that pay the most and have a lifelong impact on women's incomes. In and of itself, one Barbie doll remark would not merit that kind of backlash. But the thing is this: Barbie was part of the much larger picture where the sexist math stereotype popped up all over the place—in comedians' jokes, the packaging of children's science and math toys, movies, advertising, children's storybooks, math books at school, *and even in how girls described themselves.* That's why it was important to shut Barbie up, which Mattel did. The company recalled the doll and deleted the sexist math remark from the tiny little voice box in the new version of the doll.[1]

Society has become more sensitized to stereotypes and myths that affect women; racial, ethnic, and religious minorities; people with different mental or physical abilities; and individuals who do not identify as heterosexual. These days, most of us—especially if we are members of a stereotyped group—realize that false beliefs about certain groups of people are hurtful and harmful.

In dismantling stereotypes for the greater good, at least three things have to happen. First, we have to be able to recognize the falsehoods and stereotypes about particular groups. Sounds simple enough, but here's the thing: That is really hard to do when those beliefs are deeply ingrained throughout society and when they have become so ordinary that they barely attract our attention. It's also harder to recognize the falsehoods when we are not members of the group that is being targeted and discriminated against. Only when we reach the point where we can recognize the stereotypes and openly admit that they exist can we take the second step. We must figure out *where* and *how* those ideas are being reinforced and promoted. Sometimes this is easy, as in advertisements that portray women as mindless dimwits. Sometimes it's trickier, as in children's storybook pictures where all the human characters just happen to be white or where all the "mommy" animal characters are taking care of the children and preparing meals while the "daddies" are away doing what all dads, including human ones, are *supposed* to do: earning the family's "income."

Third, we must identify which policies, laws, and practices are discriminatory. Then we must have the courage and perseverance to change them, even if they don't seem to be harming us personally. This is worth repeating: We make more progress in eliminating stereotypes and discrimination when people who are not members of those groups join in, speak out, and work for change. This means, in the case of fathers, women should be as concerned and as active as men. Eliminating stereotypes and discrimination is a lot like pulling weeds. If we just yank off the top parts and leave the roots intact, we've accomplished nothing—except the short-lived feeling that we've solved the problem. And the more people are working together to yank out the roots, the better.

Now we're ready to discuss the stereotypes and discrimination affecting the group we are going to discuss in this book: Fathers. It has been easier to recognize stereotypes and discrimination against other groups than to recognize that we're doing the same thing to fathers. Why? In part, it's because discrimination against other groups is more obvious, for example, Blacks not being welcome at predominantly White schools or companies not hiring women for certain types of jobs. Many people then might wonder: What discrimination against fathers? What stereotypes hurt dads? How is sexism working against fathers or their children? And that's the goal of this book: to teach us how to recognize these false stinky beliefs and stereotypes about fathers when we come across them. Or at the very least, to turn up the volume of our "stink" alarm systems when we see, read, or hear insulting things about fathers that might not smell quite right and that require a little more sniffing.

On that note, take a minute to study the currency, relevance, authority/accuracy, and purpose (CRAAP) checklist in Box 1.1.[2] This checklist was designed by a University of California librarian to teach students how to think more critically and rationally. It has been widely used in public schools and colleges. These CRAAP questions help us "sniff out" the kinds of assertions, claims, and supposed "research" that should smell a little off to us when we first run across them—the stinky things that, if we fail to sense them, make us suckers for stereotypes.

Box 1.1 The CRAAP test: Currency, relevance, authority/ accuracy, and purpose[2]

Currency —the timeliness of the information
When was it published or last updated?
Have newer articles been published?
Is this a topic where information changes rapidly?

Reliability
Are there statement you know to be false?
Was the information reviewed by experts before publication?
Was it published in an academic journal?
What citations support the authors' claims?
What do other people say about the topic?
Can you verify the information from other sources?

Authority/Accuracy—the source of the information
Who is the author, the publisher, and the sponsor of the information?
What are the author's credentials and organizational affiliations?
How well-qualified is the author to write on this topic?
Did any organization sponsor or commission this article?

Purpose—the reason the information exists
Is the purpose to sell? Persuade? Entertain? Inform?
Are there political, cultural, ideological religious, or personal biases?
Are alternative points of view presented?
Does the author use strong or emotional language?

UNTIL DEATH DO US PART

How long do the stereotypes about fathers hold us in their grasp? Don't most of us, as children or as parents, outgrow them and see them for what they are? Unfortunately, certain aspects of our father stereotypes have a long shelf-life. In fact, they don't have any expiration date at all. For example, let's assume we fall for the belief that men are inferior to women when it comes to nurturing and comforting others, expressing or being in touch with their feelings and other people's feelings, and empathizing or communicating with other people. This would then mean we believe that, from the time they first become fathers to the time they are elderly men whose children are in their 50s or 60s, fathers are lacking—lacking the ability to bond closely with those they love, to share their deepest feelings, to ask for or to give comfort during the most difficult times. Those beliefs tend to influence what children and fathers *of all ages* expect from one another and how they relate to each other, from birth to death. Until death do us part.

In the same way that many young girls and women once believed the demeaning, disempowering stereotypes about females, plenty of young boys and men are still held captive by these false beliefs about how males supposedly feel and behave in their closest relationships—relationships with their wife, children, and their own elderly parents. From a child's birth to a father's death, it is heartbreaking that many of our baseless beliefs about men and relationships prevent those relationships from being all they might have been.

THE CON GAME: HOW WE ARE DUPED AND DUPE OURSELVES

If many of our beliefs about fathers are either completely false or are gross exaggerations and distortions of the research, then how did we get conned into believing them? Fortunately for us, researchers have spent decades answering that question—not specifically about fathers, but about how stereotypes get started and how the human brain tricks us into believing things that are not true. Certain findings from this huge body of research are especially useful in helping us figure out how we get hoodwinked into believing so many myths about fathers—and how our own brains even play a part in that hoodwinking.[3–7]

Why do we need to know about this research? Because if we don't want to be conned again into believing falsehoods and half-truths about dads (or about any other group of people), we need to know how we got conned in the first place. As the old saying goes, "fool me once, shame on you. Fool me twice, shame on me." More bluntly put, "there's a sucker born every minute." We can consider the following brief summary of this large body of research to be an "anti-sucker" training kit. On that note, the CRAAP test gives us a pretty good overview of what researchers have been telling us for decades about ways we can reduce the odds of being manipulated into believing things that aren't true.

Let's start with the most common trap: Repeatedly being bombarded by the same message, especially when the same one or two studies or statistics are cited over and over again. When the message or the belief is repeated often enough over a long enough time, people tend to fall for it. We don't question it because we've heard it so often that "it must be true." Social media, commercials, jokes, and TV programs are all part of the process.

Another trap is being told that "the research" or "the statistics" prove something to be true when in fact it is not true.[8] Some of the most common ways to mislead people with statistics and research are to report only the data that support one point of view (known as "cherry picking"), to overlook serious flaws in certain studies by reporting them as if they are trustworthy, to use outdated or extremely small studies, and to generalize findings from only a few studies as if they applied to large groups of people. Or research findings are reported out of context to achieve the desired goal. For example, thousands of people might die in one earthquake and the resulting tsunami. This generates worldwide attention. But that statistic alone shouldn't be used to argue that earthquakes are a major cause of death when far more people die every year from drinking contaminated water or not being vaccinated. Then too, vague words like "majority" can be misleading because they can mean as little as 51% or as much as 99%. Also, when rankings are being reported, there can be very large or very small differences between each rank. This can mislead us to believe that whatever is ranked #1 is three times larger or three times more important than whatever is ranked #3. Or if something is ranked #10, we might dismiss it as relatively unimportant unless we know that 500 items were being ranked.

We're also much more likely to accept information as trustworthy, including research findings, that reinforce what we already believe—a situation known as confirmation bias. As long as the information confirms what we already believe, it sticks to us and sticks *with* us like Velcro. But when the information flies in the face of what we already believe, we do whatever it takes to reject it. We question the source, demand more data, criticize every aspect of the study, or dismiss it outright. We see this repeatedly with conspiracy theories or news about our preferred political figures. No matter how often or how convincingly accurate information or reasonable ideas are presented to us, it slides right off our brain like a fried egg on a Teflon pan. Will the very best research and the most reliable information stick with us or not—Velcro or Teflon? It largely depends on what we believed to begin with.

We also tend to put too much trust in the people who are presenting the information to us instead of questioning what they are telling us. Popular podcasters, speakers, TV hosts, columnists, and bloggers have a lot of persuasion power, even when what they are saying fails the CRAAP test. That's not especially surprising. The surprising part is *how* they go about persuading— or conning—us. Persuasive people often rely on compelling, personal, dramatic stories that arouse our emotions more than they rely on data and research. These emotional stories not only make a bigger impression on us than the research does they also stick with us longer. Never hesitant or ambivalent, persuasive people always come across as confident—hence the term "con" artist. There are no gray areas when "con" artists are making their sales pitch. And their pitched message is always simple, straightforward, and certain. No gray areas. Game over.

Persuasive people have also mastered the KISS principle—Keep It Simple, Stupid. By presenting information in overly simplistic ways, persuasive people give us the "baby food" versions that are easier to swallow. The more complicated ideas and explanations with nuances, contradictions, and uncertainties—the kind that scholars and serious commentators rely on— are harder for us to digest and to swallow.

The KISS principle also takes advantage of our brain's weaknesses: the need for consistency and simplicity. The human brain seeks order and tries to eliminate chaos. The brain gravitates toward simple, final, clear-cut data and answers, even though important issues and our relationships with other people are often, in reality, complex, inconsistent, contradictory, irrational, ambivalent, and unanswerable. The brain also wants all incoming ideas and experiences to fit together seamlessly with its existing ideas and previous experiences. These all sound harmless and easy enough, except for the glitches: First, new "data" and new experiences streaming into our brains often clash with what is already stored there. This essential evolutionary characteristic of the brain enables us to learn new things, change our behavior accordingly, and survive as a species. Still, when these "brain clashes" occur, we feel unsettled. Second, the incoming pieces of information and new experiences are often contradictory, ambivalent, and only randomly connected to each other, if at all. When these things happen—as they inevitably do—the brain is not a happy camper. That's when we experience an unpleasant, unsettling feeling called "cognitive dissonance." We feel rattled, annoyed, confused, and out of kilter because things are not fitting together in a consonant, easy, predictable way. And what does the brain do to get rid of that irritating dissonance? It dupes us by manipulating the data *and* re-working certain aspects of our memories to force everything to fit together in a neat, consonant way. Worse yet, as the brain plays around with our memories and reshapes them into a rationale, predictable "story," we can literally "remember" things that never happened to us.[9,10]

Sadly too, we can fool ourselves into believing things about whole groups of people because we rely too much on our own personal experiences. In cases where your experiences just happen to be representative of the bigger picture, there's no harm done. For example, if half of the people you have ever known spent some time living apart from their dads when they were growing up, you might assume that about half of American children live apart from their dads at some point. And in this case, you would be right. That is exactly what national statistics show. But if your father cheated on your mother, then married a very young woman, and never paid a penny in child support, you would be flat out wrong to assume that this is how most divorced dads behave. We'll have more on these two beliefs in later chapters. The point here is this: We're on shaky ground when we make judgments and stereotype whole groups of people based only on our personal experiences—which unfortunately we often do.

As we will see throughout this book, we have often been misled—or have misled ourselves—into embracing many demeaning, demoralizing, and discouraging beliefs about fathers. As we dismantle each of those stereotypes and falsehoods, we free ourselves to see fathers as individuals who deserve more than being cast into a stereotyped group.

THE BLAME GAME

Having seen how we can be duped, and can dupe ourselves, into embracing baseless beliefs about fathers (or any group), we have to confront still another human weakness: Our tendency to blame other people. Whether in real life or in the imaginary world of movies and TV shows, when there's a crime, we want to catch the villain. We're all stirred up. We're in a hurry to find out "who done it." We want answers and we want them fast. The "gotcha" moment is so satisfying, isn't it? And who isn't thrilled when the guilty verdict is dramatically announced and the judge doles out the punishment? Of course, we'd also like to know what the criminal's motives were—greed, jealousy, or revenge? We need closure: motive, villain, jury verdict, and punishment. Case closed. Sigh of relief.

What most of us can't tolerate is a crime—in real life or in make-believe land—where the outcome is uncertain. We never find out "who done it." We have several suspects, but not enough convincing evidence or motives. Or it's a hung jury. Or, given the circumstances of the case, we're left wondering what a "fair" punishment should be. We don't like situations like these because we don't get to enjoy the peaceful feeling that comes with having closure—and closure is what the human brain craves.

But whatever way the dramas of fiction or real life turn out, there's a catch: When we're in a too much of a hurry to get catch the bad guys or when we're really stirred up about the particular crime, we might end up arresting the wrong person. And when it is a real-life crime, and we happen to know the victim—especially if we feel we are the victims—we're even less likely to have a clear view of a complex situation. So, in the end, the real villains go free and, in this day and age, live to tweet, podcast, or politic another day. If we'd been less riled up, hurried, or personally involved, we might not have made so many mistakes: overlooking important clues, following the wrong leads, and—the worst mistake of all—assuming we already know who committed the crime before the investigation really gets under way.

What does any of this have to do with fathers? A lot, as it turns out. When we start with negative beliefs about any group—in this case, fathers—we are more likely to assume those people will be the "bad guys" in the crimes. In this book, we're not referring to actual crimes like robbery, embezzlement, and Ponzi scams. In this book, we're going to discuss "crimes" that revolve around topics like the division of childcare and housework, child support payments, and the causes of divorce. As we will see, based on stereotypes and false beliefs about fathers, many of us assume that fathers are going to be the "villains" and mothers are going to be the "victims"—an assumption we make before our investigation even begins. But not in this book. Instead, we will be looking for explanations that lie at the root of the crimes and following those roots to the vast network that contribute to the crimes.

THE DETECTIVE HUNT

In this book, we will conduct our own detective hunt in solving, not one but a series of "crimes." The crimes are the damaging stereotypes, baseless beliefs, and subtle to not so subtle forms of discrimination that work against fathers and their children. The victims are the millions of children, fathers, and mothers who are being hurt by false beliefs and misleading stereotypes about fathers. We already know things are going to get complicated because there is more than one bad guy. In fact, the situation we're facing is similar to dealing with a syndicated mob that commits all kinds of crimes—from barely noticeable unreported incidents to front-page news. We're going to have our hands full because we have to figure out how each situation where people got hurt is connected to the baseless belief or stereotype that set the "crime" in motion to begin with. Fortunately, we are not naive rookies. We are pros. We will dig deeper until we discover who the accomplices are and who is working behind the scenes planting the seeds, planning, setting up the fall guys, and confidently believing they will never get caught. By the end of this book, together we will have enjoyed more than one "gotcha."

After our case is closed, being the extraordinary detectives that we are, we will go one step farther. We will help our friends, families, and communities take steps to prevent future crimes of that sort—and to protect themselves in the meanwhile from being the victims *or* the villains. We will also work in whatever ways we can to bring about changes in the laws, policies, practices, and attitudes that contributed to those acts that have hurt so many people. In regard to the case to which we have been assigned, we are always mindful that we are working on behalf of millions of children, fathers, and mothers.

REFERENCES

1. Firestone D. While Barbie talks, G.I. Joe goes shopping. *New York Times*. December 31, 1993.
2. Blakeslee S. The CRAAP test. *LOEX Q East Mich Univ.* 2004;31:30–35.
3. Chabris C, Simons D. *The Invisible Gorilla: And Other Ways Our Intuitions Deceive Us.* Crown; 2010.
4. O'Connor C, Weatherall J. *The Misinformation Age: How False Beliefs Spread.* Yale University Press; 2019.
5. Rosling H, Rosling O, Rosling A. *Factfulness: Ten Reasons We're Wrong about the World and Why Things Are Better than You Think.* Flatiron Books; 2018.
6. Kahneman D. *Thinking, Fast and Slow.* Farrar, Straus and Giroux; 2011.
7. Gelles R. The politics of research: The use and misuse of social science data. *Fam Court Rev.* 2007;45:42–51.
8. Best J. *Damned Lies and Statistics: Untangling Numbers from the Media, Politicians and Activists.* University of California; 2001.
9. Sabbagh C. *Remembering Our Childhoods: How Memory Betrays Us.* Fireside; 2010.
10. Loftus E. *The Myth of Repressed Memory.* St. Martin's; 1996.

AMERICAN FATHERS AND CHILDREN

DOI: 10.4324/9781003324003-2

Since this book is all about myths and stereotypes that hurt children's relationships with their fathers, let's start by getting a clearer picture of American children's family situations. How likely is it that children are living apart from their dads? Which children spend a part, or almost all, of their childhood living apart from him? Are there any ways to predict which dads are most likely to be separated from their children? How do American families stack up against families in other rich countries in terms of situations that lead to father-absent families?

How many children are we talking about here? There are currently about 300 million adults in the U.S. and nearly 75 million children under the age of eighteen.[1] So when we talk about factors that affect fathers' relationships with their children, we're talking about millions of Americans. As we will see, race and ethnicity are closely linked to whether children will spend the first eighteen years of their lives living with their dads. This means we need to be up-to-date on the racial makeup of America. A little under half of American children are white (non-Hispanic). About one-third are Hispanic and about half that number (15%) are Black. Only 5% are Asian American and only 1% are Native American. That might not be surprising news. But this probably will be: Only a little over half (55%) of American kids spend all eighteen years of childhood living in the same home with their father.[2] Let's restate that: The typical American child nowadays has about a 50% chance of living apart from dad.

Why such a high number? Because so many couples who once said "I do" eventually say "I don't." Only about 60% of parents are married when they have kids. Nearly half (45%) of those marriages end in divorce. Then there are 40% of parents who are not married. A whopping 80% of those relationships end, typically when the children are still young. For example, before their children reach the age of nine, more than 20% of married parents and 50% of unmarried parents have separated.[2]

Box 2.1 Are you fooling yourself? American families

Which of the following are true for most Americans?

1. Most men are fathers by the time they are 20.
2. About 80% of dads live in the same home with their children.
3. Divorce rates are higher for people in metropolitan areas.
4. About 40% of parents are not married.
5. About one in ten fathers are raising children on their own.

Which children are the most likely to end up living in a fatherless home? And after their parents' break up, who are these children living with? How do parents' educations, incomes, race, and religion come into play?

WHO ARE AMERICA'S CHILDREN LIVING WITH?[1]

Table 2.1 America's families: Who are children living with?*

54%	Mom and dad	Married
7%	Mom and dad	Not married
12%	Mom and stepdad	
2%	Mom and her boyfriend	
12%	Mom, single	Divorced from dad
12%	Mom, single	Never married to dad
1%	Dad, single	Divorced from mom
1%	Dad, single	Never married to mom
1%	Dad and stepmom	
½ %	Dad and his girlfriend	
4%	Neither parent (usually grandparents)	

* Rounded up to the nearest whole.

Slightly more than half (55%) of American children are living with their married parents. Another 7% live with their parents, but the parents aren't married. The more startling number is this: One out of four children lives with a single mother. If you look at the specific numbers in Table 2.1, you can see what this adds up to for children and their fathers. Children almost always (90%) spend their entire childhood in the same home with their mom. But only 60% of them spend their entire childhood in the same home with their dad.[1]

So what? Why should this matter? It matters because fathers who live with their children can create more supportive, loving, and involved relationships with their kids. And those are the kinds of relationships that benefit children throughout their lives. What benefits? To name a few, well-fathered children have higher high school and college graduation rates, better physical health, less delinquency, drug and alcohol use, teenage pregnancy, depression and anxiety, and better relationships with their romantic partners, including lower divorce rates. We will dive deeply into all these benefits in the next few chapters. For now, let's focus on the disturbing fact that so many children are spending years—or all—of their childhood living apart from their fathers.

Can we predict which children and fathers are most likely to end up separated from each other? Yes, we can. Why should we care? Because if we pay attention to those predictive factors, especially before couples have children, we have a better shot at reducing the odds that fathers and children will eventually be living apart.

FATHER ABSENT HOMES: RACE AND INCOME

Let's start by looking at the parents' incomes and their race or ethnicity. Here's where those statistics on race come in handy. Remember that almost half (45%) of the children under eighteen are either Black or Hispanic. You're going to see why that matters shortly.

Before looking at incomes, we have to understand the meanings of three terms: average, mean, and median. Why? Because we might be duped into believing things that aren't true. Take Hiram Jones, for example. He drowned because he didn't understand these terms. Hiram had to get across a river that didn't look particularly dangerous. He couldn't swim, but he wasn't worried. He was 6 feet tall. People told him that the "average" depth of the river was only 3 feet. No big deal for someone Hiram's height. With his head held high, he confidently waded right into that river. Stay tuned to find out why he drowned—and to find out why you can get in over your head, so to speak, when you're hearing the words mean, median, and average.

The words "mean" and "average" are synonymous. The mean or average is the mathematical number that we get when we add all the numbers together and then divide by the total number of entries. Take the incomes of 10 families, for example. One very rich family earns 5 million dollars. Four families earn $50,000 and 5 families earn a meager $20,000. Take a minute to figure out what the average or mean income is for this group. Got it? It's $530,000. Wow. What a wealthy group. But you know that isn't true because you were able to see each of family incomes. If someone had told you that the mean or average income for these ten families was $530,000, what would you need to ask to get to the truth? You would need to know the median income.

The median is the point where half of the families (or whatever is being measured) earn more than that amount and half of them earn less than that amount. To calculate this number, you arrange all the incomes from smallest to largest and then decide where the hypothetical mid-point would be between the two numbers closest to the middle. In our hypothetical example, the median income would be $35,000 because five of the ten families earned $20,000 and the other five earned above $50,000. The midway point between $20,000 and $50,000 is $35,000. If you have the median and the mean, you clearly see what's going on. These ten families are not rich. The one multi-millionaire's income is throwing the whole picture out of whack.

Poor dead Hiram Jones didn't understand this concept. Turns out the median depth of the river was 20 feet. Even though most sections of that river were just a few feet deep, the deepest sections skewed the mean (average). And that was enough to sink tall, confident Hiram.

Now that we understand the difference in mean and median incomes, we return to the question: How well do family incomes predict whether children and their fathers will live apart while the kids are growing up? Pretty well, as it turns out. Take a minute to study Table 2.2.[2] Which children have the most well-educated, richest parents? Which are the most likely to have parents who are married when the children are born? You already know that unmarried parents are far more likely to split up than married parents. So which children are probably going to spend their entire childhood living with their dad? The answer to all these questions is the same: Asian Americans. As the figures in Table 2.2 show, parents' incomes, educational levels, and being married are all linked. Highly educated parents will earn the most money and most of them will be married when they have kids. This means the fathers who are most likely to live with their kids throughout childhood are college-educated, higher income, married dads.

Race and ethnicity are closely linked to a parent's education, income, and marital status when the children are born. So which racial group has the highest percentage of father-absent homes? African American. And which

Table 2.2 Household incomes: education, race, and non-marital births[1-3]

	Living in Poverty (%)	Parents Never Married (%)	College Educated Parents (%)	Household Income Median-Halfway Point
Asian Am.	9	15	70	$95,000
White	10	30	50	$75,000
Hispanic Am.	25	50	30	$55,000
African Am.	33	75	27	$45,000

has the lowest? Asian American. The other disturbing fact is that children who are living apart from their dads are also the most likely to be living in poverty. These children are not only father-deprived they are also income deprived. For reasons we'll explore later in this book, that is a double whammy for children.

Let's take a closer look at children's families. Keep in mind that the Census Bureau's term "household" refers to households that have no children as well as those who have a large number of children. Also remember that the "median" income simply means that half of the incomes fell above that point and half fell below it. As Table 2.2 shows, almost all (85%) Asian American parents are married and the vast majority (70%) are college educated. Half of these households have a total income above $95,000. At the other extreme, most (75%) African American parents are not married and half of their total household incomes fall below $45,000. This means that Asian American children are usually the most fortunate in terms of having married, higher-income parents. And non-Hispanic white children fall somewhere in between the other racial groups, with most (70%) of them being married and about half of them being college educated.

What's the point of all these statistics? Just this: We can generally predict which children will spend their entire childhood living in the same home with their dad by looking at his educational level, his income, his race, and whether he was married to their mother when they were born.

FATHER ABSENT HOMES: THE COLLEGE FACTOR

Why is having parents who are college-educated such a strong predictor of whether children will live with their dad throughout childhood? And how strong a predictor is it? Parents without a college degree are nearly twice as likely (55%) as those with a college degree (30%) to end up divorced.[3] It might be tempting to assume that colleges teach people the skills they need to create strong marriages that can withstand the stress and strain of raising children. But that's a real stretch, though it might make a great college sales pitch. In reality though, two of the main reasons why children with college-educated parents have a chance of growing up in the same home with their dad are their parents' age and income.

Let's hone in on a really brainy factor—the brain. The human brain does not become fully mature until a person is almost thirty years old.[4] Going to college doesn't speed up that physiological timetable. Our ability to make rational, well thought-out decisions, and to control our immediate, emotion-driven impulses doesn't reach its peak until the very end of our brain development. Why? Because the part of the brain that takes the longest to reach maturity is the pre-frontal cortex that controls our irrational, impulsive, emotion-driven impulses. When people in their early to mid-20s are making decisions about getting married or having children, their brains are literally not functioning at full capacity. And that is why a college education gives young adults an edge. Young adults who are busy getting their educations are generally too pre-occupied to be getting married, let alone having kids. A college education gives a person extra years for the brain to reach full maturity, putting the brakes on our making stupid, life-changing decisions. The stages and rates of brain maturation result from thousands of years of evolution. And those stages and rates hold true whether our day job is studying for college exams, hunting saber-toothed tigers, or brokering mergers and acquisitions.

How different are the choices that college-educated and less-educated parents make? College-educated parents typically wait to have their first child until the wife is around thirty-one—nearly seven years later than less educated couples. Because the majority of Americans do not have a college education, most couples have their first child when the mother is 26. Still, because more women are now getting a college education, this is four years later than it was two decades ago.[5] Since educational levels vary from state to state, and since people in metropolitan areas are more educated than those in rural areas, there can be vast differences in how old the parents are when they have their first child. Here's one striking example. In San Francisco, women have their first child, on average, when the mother is 31. But in Todd County, South Dakota, or Zapata County, Texas, most women have their first child at twenty.[6]

The point here about education, especially a college education, is this: The less educated people are, the younger they usually are when they have kids, the lower their incomes, and the more likely they are to separate. And then? Then more of these fathers and children end up living apart. Further complicating and often undermining these father-child relationships, these dads are relatively young with low to modest incomes. To top it all off, the dad is often still at an age where the most rational part of his brain has not yet fully developed—because of his age, not because of his education. Keep in mind (no pun intended) that this is also probably true for the brain development of the relatively young mother of his children—the person he has to negotiate with for fathering time since they are no longer living together. And that opens up a whole other can of worms that we will be discussing in future chapters: how father myths and stereotypes work against fathers who are no longer living with the mother of their children.

Hopefully, you can see why these seemingly boring statistics about parents' levels of education are important. These statistics give us answers to the question: Which children and fathers are at greatest risk of living apart? And what factors contribute to their being able to maintain and strengthen their relationships? Boxes 2.1 and 2.2 can help you assess your beliefs.

RELIGION AND FATHER ABSENT FAMILIES

Box 2.2 Are you fooling yourself? Stable Marriages

Which of these are true for most Americans?

1. Religious adults are the least likely to divorce.
2. About half of college-educated people end up divorced.
3. Gay and lesbian parents are the most likely to divorce.
4. Catholics divorce less often than atheists.
5. Politically conservative people are the least likely to divorce.

When we're trying to predict which children will eventually be separated from their fathers, what role does religion play? Are children with more religious parents the luckiest? Is it generally true that "the couple that prays together, stays together"? Not so very much actually.

The most conservative religious groups have the highest rates of divorce and the highest rates of children born to unmarried parents.

These parents also tend to have the least education and lowest incomes. By now, you can probably anticipate the next question: When it comes to their parents' religious affiliations, which children are most likely to live apart from their dads? The answer is children whose parents hold the most conservative religious beliefs. Since "birds of a feather flock together," it's no surprise that college-educated people gravitate toward the more secular religions, and less educated people gravitate toward the most conservative religions.[7,8]

Consider these specific examples.[7,8] Roughly one-third of Evangelical Christians are divorced and only 10% have a college degree. In contrast, only 2% of Jews, Mormons, and atheists are divorced and nearly 60% are college graduates. On the college degree ladder, Hindus (77%) and Unitarians (67%) are at the top, and Baptists (19%) and Evangelical protestants (10%) at the bottom. Of course, people living in some states are much more religious than those in other states. Remember, parents' religious affiliations, educations, and incomes are closely linked to whether they are married when they have children and whether the mother and father's relationship lasts. Given this, which part of the country do you think has the highest percentage of children living apart from their fathers? Hint: Which part of the country is the poorest, least educated, and most religious? Answer: The South. The six most religious states and 13 of the 17 poorest states are all located in the South.[9]

INTERRACIAL MARRIAGES

What about children whose parents do not belong to the same race? Are they any more likely than other kids to wind up in a father-absent home? Yes, but only slightly.[10] About 40% of interracial couples divorce, compared to 30% of same-race couples. Most interracial marriages are between white and Hispanic Americans, followed by non–Hispanic white and Asian Americans. In fact, half of American-born Hispanics marry outside their race, as do more than a third of Asian Americans. The biggest increase, though, has been for African Americans, whose interracial marriages have tripled since 1980 to nearly 20%. Interestingly, nearly 30% of black college-educated men marry outside their race, compared to only 10% of black college-educated women. Overall though, college graduates are no more or less likely to intermarry than are less educated adults. In any case, the parents' education, income, and race are much stronger predictors than interracial marriage of whether children will spend any time in a father absent-home.

LESBIAN AND GAY PARENTS

We might also wonder whether children whose parents identify as lesbian, bisexual, or gay have any greater chance of living apart from their father. Keep in mind that relatively few Americans identify as LBGQ. Based on 2021 surveys with more than 12,000 adults, just over 7% of Americans over the age of 18 identify as LBGQ. More specifically, 4% of Americans are bisexual, and most of them are, or will be, married to or living with a person of the opposite gender. Another 0.7% are transgender, 1% are lesbians, and 1.5% are gay men.[11]

Anyway, nearly 300,000 children are living with an LGBT parent, most of whom (60%) are married to their same-sex partner. Most (70%) of these children are either adopted or born through assisted reproductive technology using donated sperm or donated eggs. The other third were born while their biological father and mother were married or living together and later separated. Since same-sex marriages are generally as stable as heterosexual marriages, these children are just as likely to be living in a two-parent home with their two fathers or with their two mothers.[12,13]

FATHER-ABSENT HOMES: WHERE AMERICA STANDS

The fact that so many American children spend part, or almost all, of their childhood living apart from their father is troubling enough by itself. But there's another unsettling reality that further disadvantages American kids. Compared to the 36 most economically advanced nations on the planet, American children are the poorest. This is so shameful that it bears repeating: America has a higher percentage of children living in poverty than the 36 countries with the most wealth. Almost 20% of American children live in poverty. By contrast, in 11 of the 36 countries, fewer than 10% of the children live in poverty. In Denmark and Finland, the rate plummets to 4%. Keep in mind that the U.S. is second to last even though it is richer than many of the other 36 countries.

What's going on here? And what does this have to do with fathers? The answer is fairly simple and straightforward. The U.S. chooses to spend far less money than other countries spend for programs that alleviate poverty, especially childhood poverty.[14] For example, Denmark and Finland spend close to 20% of their gross national product on social programs for the poor, compared to only 12% in the U.S. As for fathers, in other economically advanced countries, when children are not living with their fathers, they are far less likely to live in poverty.[15] This means that it is even more devasting for American kids to be living apart from their fathers. They not only have the disadvantage of being father deprived, they are also economically deprived.

In this sense then, the myths and stereotypes that damage children's relationships with their fathers are especially important in the U.S. because so many children are living apart from their dads and living in poverty.

CONCLUSION

While these figures and statistics may seem dry and boring, it's a mistake to ignore or downplay them because they make a very disturbing point: The majority of American children spend part—or almost all—of childhood living apart from their fathers. Because these children's relationships with their fathers are more complicated, more fragile, and more likely to fall apart over time, they are especially vulnerable to being damaged by our society's negative beliefs, unfounded assumptions, and demeaning stereotypes about fathers. If these children lived with their fathers in the same home, they would at least have the first-hand, day-to-day evidence that the myths do not apply to *their* dads.

It's the day-to-day interactions with other people that help us question—and then hopefully reject—the negative stereotypes and damaging notions we have about certain groups of people. Take racism or homophobia. In college, listening to lectures, taking tests, and writing term papers on those topics generally will have far less impact than having a roommate or teammate of a different race or sexual orientation. Or take the workplace. All those sensitivity training sessions aren't nearly as likely to change our racist or homophobic attitudes and behavior as much as working closely with co-workers whose sexual orientation or race differs from our own. It's the frequent contact—the in-your-face evidence—that undermines and destroys the stereotypes.

In the remainder of this book, we unpack the demeaning myths and unfounded stereotypes that complicate and weaken children's relationships with their dads. The goal is to support and strengthen fathers' relationships with their kids, especially in those families where the children and their dads are living apart.

ANSWERS TO THE QUIZZES

Box 2.1   1, 2 and 3 are false
Box 2.2   All of them are false

REFERENCES

1. Shrider E. Income and poverty in the U.S.: 2020, Census Bureau, Report # P60–273, 2021.
2. Livingston G. *The Changing Profile of Unmarried Parents*. Pew Research Center; 2018:1–5.
3. NCES. *National Household Education Survey and Parent Involvement*. 2018. www.nces.ed.gov/nhes.

4. Somerville L. Searching for signatures of brain maturity. *Neuron.* 2016;92: 1164–1168.

5. National Vital Statistics. *Births: Final Data for 2016.* Vol 67. Centers for Disease Control, Atlanta; 2018:1–50.

6. Livingston G. *They're Waiting Longer, but U.S. Women Are More Likely to Have Children than a Decade Ago.* Pew Research Center; 2018:1–11.

7. Cooperman D. *Religious Landscape Study.* Pew Research Center; 2014.

8. Masci D. *How Income Varies among U.S. Religious Groups.* Pew Research Center; 2016.

9. Lipka M, Wormald B. *How Religious Is Your State?* Pew Research Center; 2016.

10. Bialik K. *Key Facts about Race and Marriage.* Pew Research Center; 2017.

11. Jones J. *LGBT Identification in U.S. Ticks up to 7.1%.* February 24, 2021. Gallup; 2022.

12. Walker L, Taylor D. *Same-Sex Couple Households: 2019.* ACSBR-005. Census Bureau; 2021.

13. Lau C. The stability of same sex cohabitation and marriage. *J Marriage Fam.* 2012; 74:973–988.

14. Wilson V, Schieder J. *Countries Investing More in Social Programs Have Less Child Poverty.* Economic Policy Institute; 2018.

15. OECD. OECD database. Organization for Economic Cooperation and Development; 2019. https://stats.oecd.org/index.aspx?queryid=68249.

FATHERS DON'T MATTER— AND THE EARTH IS FLAT

DOI: 10.4324/9781003324003-3

The single most powerful myth about dads can be reduced to three words: Fathers don't matter. If you think you've never been subjected to that idea, it might be because the message was packaged in softer terms. Maybe the message was easier for you to digest because it didn't sound so harsh and so absurd. So how is the message usually packaged?

Sweet versions of "dads don't matter" play on the theme "dad is just mom's sidekick." Dad is mom's helpmate, her intern in training, and her temporary fill-in. Dad means well, but without mom there to hold his hand, he is somewhat of a doofus and clueless blockhead. A stronger version of this message is that dads do matter, but—and here's the punchline—largely for their money. Indeed, we often compliment those dads who are good "providers"—which, more crassly, means "money machines." On the flip side, if a father doesn't measure up financially, he's a failure or an embarrassment as a parent, and maybe even as a husband, regardless of the loving and supportive role he might play in the lives of his children.

The other variation on "dads don't matter" is more brutal: Children don't *need* a dad. Kids can get along just fine without him as long as mom is a good parent. Presumably then, children being raised by single mothers are not missing out on anything. And single women who choose to raise a child on their own, say, for example, through sperm donation or adoption, are not depriving the child of anything. Contrast this with our attitudes toward single men who choose to raise children on their own. Indeed, some tee shirts, jokes, and greeting cards mock fathers for being nothing more than sperm donors. Imagine mocking or joking about mothers being nothing more than incubators. Even our Mother's Day and Father's Day traditions tap into the notion that dads don't matter much, certainly not compared to mothers, as you can see in Box 3.1.

Presumably in the parenting "waters," dad is nothing more than a guppy. Mom is the whale. But, as we will see in this chapter, this couldn't be further from the truth.

Box 3.1 Father's day: Second place to Mother's day

Father's Day was founded in 1910 by Sonora Smart Dodd, who was born in Arkansas. She created Father's Day in honor of her father, a Civil War veteran who raised six children alone as a widower. In 1957, U.S. Senator Margaret Chase Smith from Maine introduced a bill to create the holiday: "Either we honor both our parents, mother and father, or let us desist from honoring either one. But to single out just one of our two parents and omit the other is the most grievous insult imaginable." It was not until 1972 that President Richard Nixon established it as a national holiday.[1]

Mother's Day was declared a national holiday in 1914 by President Woodrow Wilson. The idea was created by Anna Jarvis from West Virginia after her mother died. By the early 1920s, Hallmark and other companies were aggressively selling Mother's Day cards. Jarvis was upset because she felt the holiday had become so commercialized. She even organized boycotts and was once arrested for disturbing the peace.[2] Sorry, Anna Jarvis, but in 2021 Americans spent about $25 billion on Mother's Day gifts and $16 billion on Father's Day gifts.[3]

DAD'S INCOME MATTERS MORE THAN FATHERING

Are we still sending dads the message that the greatest contribution he can make to his kids is money? Isn't that an outdated idea from the 50s? Unfortunately, that myth is alive and well. How do we know that? Let's start with the fact that American dads spend more time at work than fathers in the other rich nations. Nearly 40% of fathers spend more than 50 hours a week at work—and not just college-educated white collar dads.[4] Their long hours at work are literally making many men sick and shortening their lives. According to 200 studies conducted over two decades, people who work long hours develop more health problems and die at an earlier age.[5] And compared to people in other rich countries, more Americans—mostly men—are in chronic physical pain and more die from suicide, drugs, and drinking. More men than women suffer and die from these "deaths of despair" which helps explain why lifespans in the U.S. have gotten shorter, while lifespans in other rich countries have gotten longer.[6] American men also take fewer weeks off work for vacation and retire much later than men in other rich countries.[7]

Most fathers say they want to spend more time with their kids and less time at work. But they don't feel they have that freedom since the family's income would suffer.[8,9] Are men just imagining this is how we feel about them? No, they are spot on. American women, men, and high school students say men should earn most—or all—of the family's money?[10,11] And America is dead last in 26 advanced countries in regard to father-friendly work policies, such as paternity leaves, paid time off for childcare, and flexible hours.[7,12] How does any of this square with the pretense—or some might call it the "lie"—that we value fathering itself more than we value men as money machines? It doesn't.

Are Americans on the right track putting so much emphasis on the dad's income? If we had to choose between more fathering time with less income, or less fathering time with more income, which is best for the kids? In more crass terms, do kids turn out better if they have a rich dad? No, they do not. Except for the 20% of children who grow up in poverty, family income is *not* closely linked to children's well-being. Richer parents' children are not better off than children from less well-to-do families when it comes to their social, psychological, emotional, behavioral, or stress-related health problems. Yes, the richer family's kids generally make better grades and are more likely to graduate from college. But here's the kicker: Wealthier parents' children are more likely to abuse drugs and alcohol and to suffer from anxiety, eating disorders, and depression, as we will see.

Overall, children from richer families don't turn out better than other children. For example, family income had no impact on whether two- and three-year-olds behave securely or insecurely in studies where the children are put in stressful situations.[13] And in a national study with 21,255 kindergarten children, kids from wealthier families did not have more advanced cognitive skills and were not more well-adjusted socially or emotionally.[14] Sixth graders in low-income schools were not more likely to use drugs or to break the law than students in wealthier schools.[15] Regardless of family income, girls who had close relationships with their dads were the ones who got along best with their peers.[16] Similarly, family income And in large national samples of high school seniors in 2016, students from wealthier families were not less likely than other teenagers to drink or use drugs.[17] But here's the more startling news: Older teenagers and young adults from higher-income families are *more* likely to use marijuana, to binge drink, to be clinically depressed, to have anxiety disorders, and to cut or burn themselves on purpose.[18,19] Even at the age of 37, adults who grew up in the wealthiest families are not less likely to feel sad, nervous, restless, hopeless, or worthless than those who grew up in middle-income families.[20] In short, dad's money isn't all it is hyped up to be.

Why aren't richer fathers' children doing better than this? Because (surprise, surprise) fathering matters—and the quality of a dad's relationship with his kids has nothing to do with his income. Teenagers and young adults from wealthier families do not report feeling closer to their parents than their counterparts from less well-to-do families.[19–22] And in the national study with the 21,255 children in kindergarten, wealthier parents were no better than other parents when it came to being warm and supportive, establishing rules, or carrying through on punishments.[14] As the stories in Box 3.2 remind us, fathers don't have to be rich to have a tremendously positive impact on their daughters.

Let's not get confused here about money. Money certainly does matter for the 20% of American children who grow up in poverty. These children have more academic, emotional, behavioral, physical health, cognitive, and developmental problems than children who are not living in poverty.[24]

Box 3.2 Famous daughters and their dads

Susan B Anthony (1820–1906) leader of women's suffrage movement[21]

Susan B. Anthony's father, Daniel, believed in equal education for boys and girls and so she was educated. Her father was a political activist who opposed slavery and often had famous reformers over to their home. Not surprisingly, Susan became a prominent leader along with her best friend, Elizabeth Caty Stanton, in the movement that won American women the right to vote.

Serena and Venus Williams, international tennis champions[22]

Internationally famous tennis champions and sisters, Serena and Venus Williams, were lovingly parented, coached, and mentored by their father, Richard. As an African American dad with five daughters, Richard started teaching Serena and Venus how to play tennis when they were only five. Both sisters have acknowledged their father's role in helping them become two of the world's most famous tennis superstars—a story documented in the Academy Award winning film, *King Richard.*[23]

For example, even at the age of 37, adults who grew up in poverty, especially during the earliest years of their lives, have more psychological and physical health problems, lower incomes, and more arrests and divorces than other Americans.[20] Worse still, the overwhelming majority of poor children live in single-mother families where they have little to no contact with their dads. They are damaged not only by the absence of money, but by the absence of their father. For example, even when the incomes of certain very poor families were doubled, the children's chances of going to college only increased by a meager 2%.[25] Even in the poorest families, fathering matters.

DAD'S PARENTING STYLE CAN'T MEASURE UP TO MOM'S

One reason we might think dads don't matter very much is the belief that a man's parenting just can't measure up to a woman's. If that is true, then it stands to reason that the mother's parenting counts more and has the greatest impact on the kids.

Let's first explore the question: Do most men and women tend to parent differently? Yes, they do, though the differences are shrinking now that more moms work outside the home, which allows fathers to do more of the direct childcare at home. Take, for example, 34 studies that involved 37,300 children ages zero to twenty.[26] Mothers are more likely than fathers to comfort, soothe, and pamper their children. They come across as more nurturing than dads. Fathers, on the other hand, tend to be more direct in communicating and dealing with their children. Dads also see their children's weaknesses and strengths more clearly—and help children see themselves more realistically, without sugarcoating. Dads also tend to have higher expectations and to push children harder to meet those expectations.

The downside of a mother's parenting style is that, when carried too far, it disintegrates into coddling, pampering, and over-parenting—all of which undermine children's maturity, resilience, tenacity, and self-reliance.[27,28] Instead of allowing and encouraging children to grapple with obstacles, failures, and challenges on their own, and to pay the price for their mistakes, mothers are too quick to rescue their children and excuse their mistakes and misbehavior. This often goes hand in hand with the over-parenting known as helicopter parenting.[29] Mom hovers over the children—micro-managing everything from playdates to college applications. Here's the kicker: American mothers do more helicopter, over-parenting than mothers in 42 other countries, which leads to feeling more burned out.[30]

And this is where the dad's parenting style benefits the kids. Fathers are more likely than mothers to parent in ways that prepare children for "real" life.[26,31] Instead of putting up with too much whining, making excuses, and feeling sorry for themselves, dads encourage children to assume responsibility and *do* something to fix the situation. As the saying goes: Mothers prepare the road for the child. Fathers prepare the child for the road. Dad is like Disappointment Panda.[32] He tells children what don't want to hear, but need to hear, about themselves—and about life. Grow up. Get over it. Suck it up. If mom is sending warm and fuzzy messages, dad is sending cold and prickly wake-up calls.

The list in Box 3.3 is from a 30-item questionnaire designed to assess the kinds of parenting that teaches children to deal with challenges. This is the kind of Disappointment Panda parenting that promotes self-reliance, responsibility, and resilience. How did your parents stack up? Or, as a parent yourself, are you more of a coddler or a challenger?

Box 3.3 No coddling: The challenging parenting checklist[33]

How did your mother generally behave? And your father?

1. Pushed me to set goals
2. Asked me what I learned from my failures
3. Made me defend my opinions
4. Pushed me to resolve problem instead of just complain about them
5. Made me deal with the consequences of my decisions or behavior
6. Challenged me to discuss issues
7. Asked me to explain the reasoning behind my decisions
8. Let me make decisions even though I made mistakes
9. Asked me challenging questions that made me think
10. Encouraged me to try new things on my own

Children who are coddled pay a price.[27,28] As teenagers and young adults, they are often more prone to depression, anxiety disorders, and stress-related physical problems such as migraines, stomach aches, and insomnia. In college, these students—and too often their coddling parents—expect to be shielded from situations that might be too upsetting or unsettling for them. The bad grade, the mistake on the athletic field, and other setbacks are inflated into insurmountable catastrophes leading to a meltdown. Even though they might be straight A students attending prestigious colleges, many of them are easily toppled emotionally when stressed, challenged, or contradicted. Too often, they expect others, including their professors, to

Box 3.4 Disappointment Panda

"If I could invent a superhero, I would invent one called Disappo-intment Panda.[32] His superpower would be to tell people harsh truths about themselves that they need to hear but didn't want to accept. He would go door to door like a Bible salesman and ring doorbells and say things like, 'Sure, making a lot of money makes you feel good, but it won't make your kids love you.' He'd make our lives better despite making us feel worse. Disappointment Panda would be the hero that none of us would want, but all of us would need."

Mark Manson, author, podcaster, and comedian,
"The Subtle Art of Not Giving a F–k"

"prepare the road" for them, when what they need is a swift kick in the pants from Disappointment Panda, who is described in Box 3.4.

Can fathers ever be the coddling helicopter parents and mothers be Dis-appointment, Pandas? Yes, of course. And in some families, both parents are pandas or both are coddlers. Even though the vast majority of "helicopter coddlers" are mothers, this does not mean that the vast majority of mothers fall into that trap. Still, if we're trying to predict which parent is more likely to be Disappointment Panda, it's the dad.

DADS SPANK AND ABUSE KIDS MORE THAN MOMS DO

Because dad usually has more stringent standards and is not as willing to put up with immature, irresponsible behavior, we might fall prey to another myth: Dads are usually the ones who use corporal punishment when they have to discipline the kids. The frightening stereotype of the stern father, angry hand raised to hit or spank his child, plays into an even more terrifying belief: Fathers physically abuse their children far more other than mothers do.

Every year in the U.S. nearly 900,000 parents are reported for child abuse or child neglect (i.e. not feeding or providing medical care for the child, leaving young children alone for hours). The vast majority (80%) of these children are under the age of four. About a fourth of these cases are for physical child abuse. The rest are for neglect. Nearly 1,500 children die from this abuse or neglect each year. Who are these parents? According to national statistics, the most negligent and abusive are single mothers with more than one child, especially mothers living in poverty.[34]

But what about children whose parents are not abusive or negligent? Isn't it usually the dad who spanks or takes a switch to the kids? No. It's the mother.[35-37] In fact, in low-income families, after the father moves in with his children's single mother, her spanking and her verbal aggression toward the kids decreases by 40%.[36] Interestingly too, over the first five years of their lives, children who were spanked by their moms became more aggressive but those spanked by their dads did not.[37] Still, prestigious organizations including the American Psychological Association and the American Association of Pediatricians agree that spanking is not good for children regardless of who does the spanking. Of course, gender isn't the only factor. For example, born-again Christians, Republicans, and Southerners are the most likely to spank their children. And middle or lower-income parents are more likely to spank than richer, more educated parents.[38] The point here is that, even though dad's style of parenting is not as warm and fuzzy as mom's, dad is *not* the one who does most of the spanking. It's mom.

So how to the differences in mothers' and fathers' parenting styles affect their children? Is it true that dads don't matter—at least not nearly as much as moms do? Is dad the guppy in the parenting waters? No, he is not.

PHYSICAL HEALTH: DADS DON'T HAVE MUCH IMPACT ON CHILDREN'S PHYSICAL HEALTH, RIGHT?

Doesn't mom have the greater impact on children's physical health, especially as babies? No, she does not. Let's start with one of the most important gifts that parents can give their babies and toddlers: sleep. When children don't get enough sleep, they are much more difficult to handle. And the first six months are the hardest on parents because this is when babies have the most trouble sleeping through the night. It's no wonder that millions of frustrated parents enjoyed the book, *Go the F*ck to Sleep*: "The windows are dark in the town, child. The whales huddle down in the deep. I'll read you one very last book, if you swear. You'll go the f**k to sleep."[39]

Seeing to it that babies get enough sleep is no laughing matter. Indeed, researchers have been wide awake investigating that topic for decades. Babies and toddlers who sleep well at night are more cooperative and energetic, less fretful, aggressive, or hyperactive, and easier to soothe. They are also more mentally alert and attentive and have more advanced vocabularies than sleep-deprived babies.[40,41]

What's more eye-opening is this: Dads play a big role in how well their babies sleep. Babies and toddlers whose fathers are actively involved in their care sleep far better than babies whose fathers are relatively uninvolved.[42,43] And here's another unexpected bonus: Well-rested babies are less apt to gain too much weight and become obese by the time they are teenagers.[44] For example, preschoolers who didn't get to have their usual naps and whose nighttime sleep was reduced started eating more, especially sugary and fatty foods.[45] This research on sleep and obesity is really worth paying attention to because childhood obesity is a major health problem in the U.S.—increasing the risk of heart attacks, strokes, cancer, kidney and liver failure, damaged joints, diabetes, miscarriages, and infertility later in life.[46] Is good fathering in these first few of his baby's life one way to prevent children from growing up to be obese adults? Yes, so it seems.

The added payoff, of course, is that the more sleep the baby gets at night, the more sleep the parents get. This is a big deal—a very big deal. Well-rested adults are not only better parents to their babies they also get along better with each other than sleep-deprived, exhausted parents. Parents whose three-month-old babies woke them up several times a night were more depressed and argued more with each other than parents whose babies slept better through the night, regardless of the parents' incomes or educational levels. And as the babies got older and started sleeping better, the parents became less depressed.[47] New mothers and fathers who are sleep deprived are more likely to become clinically depressed in the first year of their baby's life.[48] And new fathers whose wives become depressed are twice as likely themselves to become clinically depressed.[49] We really need to pay attention to this: Nearly a third of new mothers *and* fathers develop symptoms of moderate to severe depression in the first year of their baby's life. And when the dad becomes depressed, he becomes less involved in taking care of the baby and the relationship between the parents deteriorates.[50] From the third trimester of the pregnancy until the baby is a year old, roughly 10% of mothers *and fathers* experience depression.[51] A sleep-deprived baby or parent is nothing to take lightly. We need to heed the wake-up call. Fathers play a very big role in their baby's physical health, much of which depends on how well the baby sleeps in those first few years.

The dad's impact on his children's health doesn't stop in infancy. Children whose fathers are loving, supportive, and actively involved in their lives are generally in better health.[31,52] They are less likely to become obese and more physically active, including organized sports. They also have fewer stress-related health problems such as headaches and stomach aches. As teenagers and young adults, they are less likely to engage in risky behaviors that lead to serious injuries or death while they are young and to serious health problems as adults. These include drinking and drug use, driving while under the influence, and contracting sexual diseases from unprotected sex. For example, in surveys at nine universities with more than 1,700 female students, women who had good relationships with their dads took fewer health risks than women those with distant or troubled relationships.[53] And in one of the few studies to look specifically at which parent has the most influence, the quality of sons' and daughters' relationships with their dads had the most impact on their weight, blood pressure, and heart rates.[54] Well-fathered daughters also have fewer health problems related to eating disorders or injuries from a physically abusive boyfriend.[55] And in national surveys with almost 68,000 American children, those living in the same home with their dad were in better health than kids in all other kinds of families, including mom and stepdad

Box 3.5 Title IX: Gender equity in education

Fathers: A girl's best friend in the fight for sports equity[59]

Herb Dempsey might be considered the king of Title IX fathers. In 2012 Herb lived in Castle Rock, WA, where girls' soccer games were shortened to 32 minutes from 80 minutes because there were no lights on the field to play at night. The nearby boys' football field, of course, was well-lighted. Herb won the battle to light up the girls' games, literally. And in Illinois, Paul Bucha, a retired Army colonel, filed a class action suit so his daughter would be allowed to swim on her high school team. She became a champion marathon swimmer and criminal law attorney. In Delaware, former major league pitcher and future manager, Dallas Green lent the name of his nine-year-old daughter, Kim, to one of the lawsuits that helped end Little League's boys-only policy. Other 2012 battles creating equity in girls' softball were also led by fathers: Ron Randolph, a firefighter in Owasso, Oklahoma, Pat Egan, a contractor in Florence, Kentucky, and Russell Johnson, a pipe fitter in Gadsden, Alabama.

families.[56] Remember that childhood and teenage obesity has become a major health problem in the U.S.—increasing the risk of heart attacks, strokes, cancer, kidney and liver failure, damaged joints, diabetes, miscarriages, and infertility later in life.[46] And children are getting fatter earlier in their lives than ever before.

Further tipping the scales, physically inactive children and teenagers are not only fatter they also have poorer cognitive skills and are more depressed than their peers.[57] So dads who help their kids maintain a normal weight are having an impact on more than their health. Even as preschoolers, children whose dads are fat and physically inactive are more overweight and inactive themselves.[58] Monkey see, monkey do. Bravo for the dads described in Box 3.5.

STRESS REGULATION: DADS DON'T AFFECT HOW CHILDREN DEAL WITH STRESS

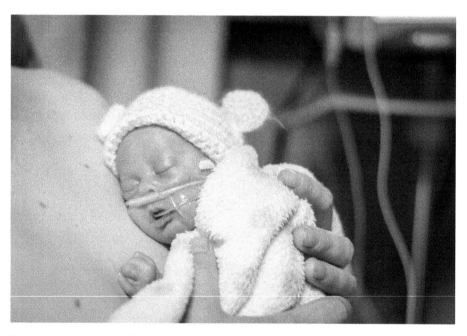

Father "Kangaroo Care" for Premature Babies

Even if we are "woke" to the research on fathers mattering when it comes to their babies' sleeping well, what about the baby's emotional and physical stress? Isn't it usually the mother who helps children learn to manage stress?

Let's start by looking at what happens when we're stressed, no matter how old we are. From the time we are born, whenever we feel stressed, our body automatically goes into "flight or fight" mode. Our blood pressure and heart rate increase. Our levels of cortisol and oxytocin—the stress-reducing hormones—get out of whack. Like the rest of us, babies and toddlers do get stressed, say, for example, when they meet a stranger or when they hear their parents screaming at each other. And their bodies go into stress mode. In small doses and for short periods, stress is a good thing. It motivates us, helps us get away from dangerous situations, and forces us to learn new skills. But when we can't get our stress under control and our bodies stay in high alert mode, our mental and physical health suffer. Chronic high stress leads to anxiety disorders, depression, high blood pressure, strokes, autoimmune diseases, and stress-related physical ailments.

The trick is learning how to regulate or reduce stress on our own. This self-regulation is a skill we learn—or don't learn—when we're babies and toddlers. Guess who is usually our first stress management instructor? Dear old dad.[60]

Let's focus first on some intriguing studies about stress and premature babies.[61-63] Traditionally, premature babies were kept physically apart from their parents, isolated in incubators where parents could only touch them for short periods of time through openings in the incubator. Then "Kangaroo Care" hopped into the picture. In this unique approach, the baby is taken out of the incubator and placed on the mother's bare chest, where she holds the infant against her, in a "pouch" so to speak, a few times throughout the day. Compared to preemies who didn't get the kangaroo care, these babies became healthier faster and had better cognitive development and better health even several years later. What was happening was this: As the mom and baby were in skin-to-skin contact for a long enough time, both of their bodies began to de-stress. Their high blood pressure and fast heart rate went down. Levels of the stress-reducing hormones, cortisol and oxytocin, became more normal. Eventually, another idea hopped onto the research scene. Maybe babies could benefit from daddy kangaroo care. And, sure enough, when fathers were allowed to be the "kangaroos," the same good things happened to the baby's body and to the dad's body. And, several years later, the preemies who had gotten the daddy kangaroo care were physically healthier and had better cognitive skills than those without the daddy care. When it came to "preemie pouches," the dads were no slouches.

Now back to the question: How do fathers help their babies manage stress—literally to change what is happening inside their baby's stressed body?[31,64,65] First, dad creates stress for the baby. What? That can't be right. Yes, dad stresses his baby by playing in challenging, unpredictable, some-what scary or risky ways. Dad tosses his baby in the air, engages in rough and tumble play, plays "boo," sneaks up on the child pretending to be a scary animal, presents the child with challenging, somewhat frustrating tasks, or allows the child to get into a somewhat risky situation (i.e. climb-ing down from a step, going down a slide). The child is entertained and joyfully excited. But this excitement comes at a price—stress. Dad has tem-porarily destabilized his baby's stress regulation system. Now it's his job to restabilize things. He does this by reassuring, soothing, and comforting the child. The baby's body returns to its normal, relaxed state. And the baby has now acquired some stress-regulation experience.

Dads also have an impact on their child's physical stress by how they interact with their wives. For example, when parents have intense arguments in front of their baby, the child's cortisol levels ramp up. Even several days later, the baby's cortisol levels are still elevated.[66] Likewise, children who grow up in high-conflict families have higher cortisol levels than children from happier, more peaceful families even years later.[67,68]

Fast forward twenty years on a child's stress and cortisol clock. Spoiler alert: This is going to be worse news for daughters than for sons. Here we go. First, daughters have more stress-related problems than sons, including: anxiety disorders, depression, autoimmune diseases, and migraines.[55] In part, this is because females have a stronger cortisol response than males do when they're stressed.[69] Their higher cortisol levels then contribute to more stress-related physical and emotional problems. Generally speaking, daughters' relationships with their fathers are not as close as their relationships with their mothers, especially if the parents are divorced.[70] The end result is that daughters who have non-existent or troubled relationships with their dads generally have higher cortisol levels and more stress-related health problems than daughters who have warm, supportive, relaxed relationships with their dads.[71,72]

Here's another fascinating father-daughter tidbit: Daughters seem to have cortisol levels similar to their fathers—regardless of whether the level is high or normal.[73] Daughters who started college (a stressful situation) with normal cortisol levels were less anxious at the end of their freshmen year than daughters who started college with higher cortisol levels. When the researchers put the fathers in a stressful situation at the time their daughters started college, dads with the more anxious daughters had higher cortisol levels than dads with less anxious daughters.

With their daughters and with their sons, fathers can be stress busters—but only if they are highly involved with their babies and toddlers in these playful, challenging, attentive ways.

DADS DON'T HAVE MUCH IMPACT ON CHILDREN'S COGNITIVE DEVELOPMENT ESPECIALLY WHEN THEY ARE YOUNG

Turning our attention from children's physical health and stress management to their cognitive development, how much do dads matter? How true is it that dads matter most only when their children are old enough to need help with school work, especially science or math-related work (just sticking with the gender stereotype festival here)? Isn't it true that dad doesn't really have much impact on his very young child's cognitive skills?

Let's start at zero—birth. From the time babies are born, they are interacting with the world around them. Those interactions are building and strengthening neural networks in the baby's brain. The more stimulation, the better. Fathers who are highly involved and spend plenty of time playing and interacting with their babies are ramping up their baby's brains. These well-fathered babies are more physically and mentally active, have longer attention spans, are more willing to tackle challenging tasks, and are more persistent in sticking with an activity. These children also have bigger vocabularies and better counting skills as toddlers.[31,60] All of this, of course, leads to more success when they start to school.

But is this true even in lower-income families where fewer dads have any college education? Yes, it is. In fact, even in single-mother families, when fathers spend time with their babies being actively, playfully, and regularly engaged, their children have better reading and math scores years later in elementary school.[74] In fact, in a national longitudinal study with 8,400 two-year-olds, the father's involvement was even more beneficial for babies in single-mother families than in married-parent families. These well-fathered toddlers had fewer sleep and eating problems, were better at calming themselves, and had better vocabularies and problem-solving skills.[75] Similarly, in 1,300 married families where half were living in poverty, children whose dads were reading bedtime stories to them at six months of age had better language skills at age three—regardless of whether the mother had read to them or not.[76] Even though both parents only had high school educations, these dads used more advanced vocabulary and asked more "what" and "why" questions to the children than the moms did. Similarly, with another group of married parents, toddlers with the involved dads had more advanced vocabularies, regardless of how involved the mother had been with them.[77] And fifth graders whose fathers were reading and singing to them when they were two to three years old had better achievement scores than those whose dads had not read or sung to them.[78] Even when babies are only three months old when their dads are highly involved with them, they had more advanced cognitive developed as two-year-olds. This held true even when the mom had been depressed and regardless of how sensitive she had been toward the baby.[79] The key for the babies in these lower-income families is the dad's active, attentive, sensitive involvement very early in their lives.

What is it, then, that dads do that benefits babies and toddlers? How is that any different from what moms generally do? Again, large part of the answer is play. Dad's play is usually more stimulating, challenging, unpredictable, and demanding. He uses more advanced vocabulary—less baby talk, more grown-up talk. Dads tease children and encourage, or sometimes gently force them to go beyond their physical or mental abilities. All of this teaches the child how to deal with frustration and failure without having a meltdown—all of which boost their cognitive and social skills.

SOCIAL DEVELOPMENT: DADS DON'T TEACH CHILDREN HOW TO COMMUNICATE OR GET ALONG WITH OTHERS THE WAY MOTHERS DO

Even if we admit that dads play a major role in their young children's cognitive development, isn't it still true that mothers are the ones who teach children how to get along with other people? After all, women have better relationship and communication skills than men. Of course, mothers will be the ones to teach those skills to their children. Right? Wrong.

Let's start with the extreme—babies who have very difficult, volatile temperaments. Unlike calmer, more even-tempered infants, these babies are extremely fretful, hard to soothe, aggressive (hitting, biting, kicking, spitting), uncooperative, and easily upset. They are exhausting and exasperating. By time they are toddlers, it's clear that they have a hard time getting along with other children. That's the bad news. Here's the good news: When fathers are actively involved with these difficult babies, their children have fewer social and behavioral problems at age five or six than when their fathers are less involved early on.[80,81]

But even babies with calm temperaments have to be taught how to regulate their emotions and control their behavior. In fact, self-regulation is one of the most important tasks we humans have to master in these first few years of our lives. If we don't learn to control our emotions and reign in our out-of-control behavior at this early age, odds are we will continue to relate to other people like, well… babies. Obviously, this doesn't go over well in making friends, getting along with teachers and employers, or succeeding at dating and marriage.

This is where fathers play such a pivotal role. Babies and toddlers whose fathers are regularly engaged with them in stimulating, challenging ways are less aggressive, have better control of their emotions, and have more mature social skills than children whose dads are less involved or less playful with them at this early age.[82-84] For example, five-year-olds who are overly anxious and withdrawn around other kids are less securely attached to their dads than kids who are sociable and outgoing.[85] Here's a real stunner: In a 16-year study that followed children from early childhood to young adulthood, young adults whose dads had been rated as highly sensitive with them as infants and toddlers felt more secure in their adult romantic relationships than young adults whose fathers had not been very sensitive parents to their babies. The mother's sensitivity toward the children as babies had no impact on their later romantic relationships.[86]

The insulting assumption that fathers aren't very good at teaching their children how to get along with other people is rooted in other demeaning beliefs about men. Men can't empathize with people the way women can. Men don't communicate as well and don't cooperate as much as women do. Put bluntly, men are inferior to women when it comes to relationships. Obviously, if we fall for this, it's easier to believe mothers are the ones who teach children how to communicate, empathize, and get along with others.

Here's the problem with that idea: It isn't true. Men are not inferior to women in these ways. For nearly half a century, research has been telling us that men are just as empathetic, just as cooperative, and just as good at communicating as women.[87–90] In fact, there are more differences among women and more differences among men than there are between men and women. As for empathy and compassion, men and boys are not less likely than women and girls to empathize or to put other people's feelings and needs ahead of their own.[91] In fact, adults who grew up in father-absent homes are less empathetic than adults who grew up in homes with their fathers.[92] If fathers are "empathy empty" and mothers are "empathy full," then why weren't the single mothers' children super empathetic since mom was the only one in charge of the parenting? We'll be exploring these myths about empathy and communicating in the next chapter. For now, the point is that there is no reason to assume that fathers won't be as good as mothers in teaching their children how to communicate, empathize, and get along with other people.

DADS SHOULDN'T DO "GIRLY" STUFF PARENTING

One of the most beneficial kinds of play for young children is imaginary play—play that requires them to create make-believe, creative conversations with another person. Imaginary play builds vocabulary, enhances creativity, and advances their social skills. The right kind of imaginary play also gives parents a chance to show their silly, goofy, childlike, emotional side—a side that children often do not get to see in their dad.

Given the importance of imaginary play, we should be troubled by this damaging myth: Dads shouldn't play dolls or engage in other "girly" games and activities. Doll play is only for mommies—and only for girls. Not only are dolls usually off limits for dad, so are other gender-stereotyped things like pretending to cook in a child-size kitchen, playing "family" with little wooden figures in their doll house, or styling his daughter's hair.

Let's get down to the nitty-gritty—the research on playing with dolls. Yes, researchers have put America's most popular doll to the test— Barbie. One group of 4- to 8-year-olds "played Barbies" with another child. Another group played a game on a tablet with another child. Two other groups played alone, either with Barbie or the tablet game. As the children played, the researchers measured the brain activity in the prefrontal cortex—the area responsible for a host of functions, including focusing our attention, predicting the consequences of our behavior, and controlling our emotions and impulsive behavior. Guess who won the brain contest? Barbie—especially playing Barbie with another child. Playing the tablet game increased brain activity, but it was no match for Barbie (though, to be honest, Barbie has not previously been well-known for her brain). Now get this: The boys' brains became just as activated as the girls' brains when they played Barbie. And that, in a nutshell, is why dads should play Barbie, not only with their daughters but with their sons.[93]

Yes, but, are dads any good at imaginary play? Isn't that really more of a mom thing? No, it's not a mom thing. Take, for example, a study with mostly Latino and African American low-income parents who were engaged in imaginative play with their two-year-olds. The toddlers whose dads were the most imaginative and playful ended up with better vocabularies in pre-kindergarten than the toddlers who had less playful, less imaginative dads. But the mom's level of playfulness had no impact.[94] Obviously, the dads got an A when it came to imaginary play.

Years ago, toy companies got the picture: Girls like to play with "boy" toys.[95] Bingo! The dollar signs lit up in their eyes. There was money to be made here. Companies stopped packaging and advertising toys for boys only. But companies have been slow to change when it comes to dads playing dolls with their children. One notable exception is Mattel corporation who launched an enormously popular, award winning 2016 advertising campaign called "Dads play Barbies."[96] The campaign slogan was "time spent in her imaginary world is time spent in her real world." The commercials showed dads—big burly guys, African American dads, the whole lot—acting silly and childlike, talking in high-pitched voices, and earnestly playing Barbie with their daughters. The award-winning campaign went viral.

Still, the idea of dads playing dolls with their kids is a hard sell. We can hope the time will come when fathers are given the freedom and permission to enjoy this kind of meaningful, beneficial play with their daughters and sons. Just as we once disapproved of girls playing with "boy" toys, someday we will joyfully allow dads to move into doll territory.

THE PARENTING CONTEST: STOP!

Who doesn't love a contest? Who won? How close was the score? We don't like a tie or a draw. We want a clear-cut winner. So maybe it's inevitable that we can't resist the temptation to rank mothers and fathers in some kind of imaginary parenting contest. Who is the winner—mom or dad? And how much have you ever bet on—or participated in—this contest? Don't do this. It is a silly and pointless contest. Why?

As we have seen, dads have a huge impact on their children from infancy on. This isn't groundbreaking news. This is old news. For decades researchers have been telling us that well-fathered children are better off with respect to grades, achievement scores, high school and college graduation rates, teen pregnancy, drug and alcohol use, delinquency, behavior at school, relationships with their peers and teachers, and their romantic relationships as teenagers and adults. These children are less likely to have eating or anxiety disorders, to be clinically depressed or suicidal, to have low self-esteem or to be easily overwhelmed by stress, failure, and life's misfortunes.[26,31,60]

We also have known for decades that children who grow up in father-absent homes have the worst outcomes.[97] We also know that if their fathers remain actively involved in their lives after their parents separate, kids have better outcomes—a topic we'll dive into in Chapter Five. In terms of cold hard cash, we also know that children whose fathers were actively involved in their lives have higher incomes as adults than children whose fathers were less involved.[98]

Sometimes fathers actually do "win" the parenting contest—and some-times mothers win. Take, for example, the father's impact on his daughter. Generally speaking, the father has more impact than the mother on the quality of the daughter's romantic relationships with men.[70] And in 220 studies involving more than 33,000 young adults from 23 nations, daughters' mental health problems were more closely linked to feeling accepted by their fathers than feeling accepted by their mothers.[99] As for the college years, for more than 1,700 female students in nine universities, on 12 different measures of risky behavior (e.g. binge drinking, having sex with a man they don't know well, using drugs), the quality of their relationships with their dads predicted their risk-taking behavior more than their relationships with their moms.[53] But the fact that fathers' have more impact on their daughters in these regards doesn't mean that fathers are more important than mothers.

The point is that it's time to call off the contest and acknowledge that mothers and fathers make equally important contributions to their children's lives. Game over. Each parent's contributions are different—not better or worse, just different. This also applies, of course, to lesbian couples and gay fathers who are raising children together. Trying to rank the parents is also silly because one parent might have more impact on the children at certain ages and because siblings have different personalities. Dad might be better at parenting Susie. Mom might be better at parenting Sam. Dad might be better than mom dealing with the kids when they're babies. Mom might deal better with them as teenagers. Who cares? As long as children feel loved and well cared for, they aren't judging their parents in some imaginary contest—no matter what the canny little critters might tell their parents when they're trying to get their way about something.

If there's a parenting contest, it's the parents—not the kids—who are probably creating and fueling it. At that point, the question is: Are you so insecure as a parent that you have to turn parenting into a competition where you have to be the winner? Don't do that. For the sake of the children, let both parents be winners—especially if the parents do not get along well or are divorced. As the ridiculous Dodo bird character in *Alice in Wonderland* proclaimed at the end of a pointless, foolish race where nobody could possibly be declared the winner: "*Everybody* has won and *all* must have prizes."[100]

REFERENCES

1. LaRossa R. *The Modernization of Fatherhood: A Social and Political History.* University of Chicago Press; 1997.
2. Collins L. Mother's day 100-year history. *Deseret News.* May 12, 2019.
3. McGinty M. *Father's Day Spending Expect to Reach All-Time High of $16 Billion.* National Retail Federation Press Release. 2019; May 30, 2021.

4. Cha Y, Weeden K. Overwork and the slow convergence in gender gap in wages. *Am Sociol Rev.* 2014;79:457–484.

5. Pencavel J. *Diminishing Returns at Work: The Consequences of Long Working Hours.* Oxford University Press; 2018.

6. Case A, Deaton A. *Deaths of Despair and the Future of Capitalism.* Princeton University Press; 2020.

7. Glass J, Andersson M, Simon R. Parenthood and happiness: Effects of work-family reconciliation policies in 22 OECD countries. *Am J Sociol.* 2016;122:886–929.

8. Parker K, Livingston G. *Seven Facts about American Dads.* Pew Research Center; 2017.

9. Harrington B, Fraone J, Lee J, Levey L. *The New Millennial Dad: Understanding the Paradox of Today's Fathers.* Boston College Center for Work & Family; 2016.

10. Dernberger BP, Pepin JR. Gender flexibility, but not equality: Young adults' division of labor preferences. *Sociol Sci.* 2020:117–132. Published online.

11. Parker K, Stepler R. *Americans See Men as the Financial Providers.* Pew Research Center; 2017.

12. Rho H, Fremstad S, Biegel J. *Contagion Nation 2020: United States Still Only Wealthy Nation without Paid Sick Leave.* Vol March, 2020. Center for Economic and Policy Research; 2020.

13. Groh A, Fearon R, van Ijzendoorn M, Bakermans M, Roisman G. Attachment in the early life course. *Child Dev Perspect.* 2017;11:70–76.

14. Gershoff E, Aber L, Raver C, Lennon M. Income is not enough: Incorporating material hardship into models of income associations with parenting and child development. *Child Dev.* 2007;78:70–95.

15. Luthar S, Latendresse S. Comparable risks at the socioeconomic status extremes: Preadolescents' perceptions of parenting. *Dev Psychopathol.* 2005;17:207–230.

16. Webster L, Low J, Siller C, Hackett R. Understanding the contribution of a father's warmth on his child's social skills. *Fathering.* 2013;11:90–113.

17. Johnston L, et al. *Key Findings on Adolescent Drug Use.* Institute for Social Research, University of Michigan; 2017:1–114.

18. Humensky J. Are adolescents with high socioeconomic status more like to engage in alcohol and illicit drug use in early adulthood? *Subst Abuse Treat Prev Policy.* 2010;5:12–20.

19. Luthar S, Barkin S, Crossman E. I can, therefore I must: Fragility in the upper middle classes. *Dev Psychopathol.* 2013;25:1529–1549.

20. Duncan G, Ziol-Guest K, Kalil A. Early childhood poverty and adult attainment, behavior and health. *Child Dev.* 2010;81:306–325.

21. Cooper I. *Susan Anthony.* Franklin Watts; 1984.

22. Williams S. *Queen of the Court: An Autobiography.* Random House; 2012.

23. Green R. *King Richard.* Warner Brothers; 2021.

24. Brooks-Gunn J, Duncan G. *Consequences of Growing up Poor.* Russel Sage Foundation; 1997.

25. Mayer S. *What Money Can't Buy: Family Income and Children's Life Chances.* Harvard University Press; 1997.

26. Jeynes W. Meta-analysis on the roles of fathers in parenting: Are they unique? *Marriage Fam Rev.* 2016;52:665–688.

27. Lukianoff G, Haidt J. *The Coddling of the American Mind*. Penguin; 2018.
28. Lythcott-Haims J. *How to Raise an Adult: Break Free of the Overparenting Trap and Prepare Your Kid for Success*. Henry Holt; 2015.
29. Fingerman K, et al. Helicopter parents and landing pad kids: Intense parental support of grown children. *J Marriage Fam*. 2012;74:880–896.
30. Roskam I, et al. Parental burnout around the globe: A 42-country study. *Affect Sci*. 2021;2:58–79.
31. Lamb M. *The Role of the Father in Child Development*. Wiley; 2010.
32. Manson M. *The Subtle Art of Not Giving a F–k*. Harper; 2016.
33. Daily R. Parental challenge: A measure of how parents challenge their adolescents. *J Soc Pers Relatsh*. 2012;25:643–669.
34. Finkelhor D. *Childhood Victimization*. Oxford University Press; 2014.
35. Hallers-Haalboom A. Wait until your mother gets home! Mothers' and fathers' discipline strategies. *Soc Dev*. 2016;24:82–98.
36. Schneider W. Relationship transition and the risk of child maltreatment. *Demography*. 2016;53:1771–1800.
37. Shawna L, Altschul I, Gershoff E. Wait until your father gets home? Mother's and father's spanking and development of child aggression. *Child Youth Serv Rev*. 2015;52:158–166.
38. Schneider W. Single mothers, the role of fathers and the risk for child maltreatment. *Child Youth Serv Rev*. 2017;81:81–93.
39. Mansbach A, Cortes R. *Go the F★★k to Sleep*. Akachic Books; 2011.
40. Licis A. Sleep disorders assessment and treatment in preschool-aged children. *Child Adolesc Psychiatr Clin N Am*. 2017;26:587–594.
41. Hoyniak C. Less efficient neural processing related to irregular sleep and less sustained attention in toddlers. *Dev Neuropsychol*. 2015;40:155–166.
42. Ayalon M. The role of the father in child sleep disturbance. *Infant Ment Health J*. 2015;36:114–127.
43. Tikotzky L, Sadeh A, Volkovich E, Manber R, Meiri G, Shahar G. Infant sleep development from 3 to 6 months: Links with maternal sleep and paternal involvement. *Monogr Soc Res Child Dev*. 2015;36:107–123.
44. Miller M. Sleep duration and incidence of obesity in infants, children and adolescents: A systematic review and meta-analysis. *Sleep*. 2018;41:244–253.
45. Mullins E, et al. Acute sleep restriction increases dietary intake in preschool-age children. *J Sleep Res*. 2017;26:48–54.
46. Hales C, et al. *Prevalence of Obesity among Adults and Youth: 2015–2016*. Centers for Disease Control & Prevention, report # 288; 2017:1–5.
47. McDaniel B, Teti D. Coparenting quality during the first three months after birth: The role of infant sleep quality. *J Fam Psychol*. 2018;26:886–895.
48. Loutzenhiser L, McAuslan P, Sharpe D. The trajectory of maternal and paternal fatigue across the transition to parenthood. *Clin Psychol*. 2015;19:15–27.
49. Ramchandani P. Postpartum depression in fathers. *Lancet*. 2005;44:144–155.
50. Paulson J, Bazemore S. Prenatal and postpartum depression in fathers. *J Am Med Assoc*. 2010;19:54–63.
51. Gross CL, Marcussen K. Postpartum depression in mothers and fathers. *Sex Roles*. 2017;76:290–305.

52. Luecken L. Nonresidential father psychological support and offspring physical health perceptions 15-years after parental divorce. *Fam Court Rev.* 59:294–308.

53. Schwartz S, et al. Perceived parental relationships and health risk behaviors in college attending adults. *J Marriage Fam.* 2009;71:727–740.

54. Niu Z. Impact of childhood parent-child relationships on cardiovascular risks in adolescence. *Prev Med.* 108:53–59.

55. Nielsen L. Father-daughter relationships: Research and issues. In: Perry A, Mazza C, eds. *Fatherhood in America.* Charles Thomas; 2016:115–152.

56. Ziol-Guest K, Dunifon R. Complex living arrangements and child health. *Fam Relat.* 2014;63:424–437.

57. Lubans D, et al. Physical activity for cognitive and mental health in youth. *Pediatrics.* 2016;138:161–182.

58. Vollmer R, et al. Investigating the relationships of body mass index and physical activity level between fathers and their preschool-aged children. *J Acad Nutr Diet.* 2015;115:919–926.

59. Wolff A. Father figures: A girl's best friend in the fight for playing time. *Sports Illus Vault.* May 7, 2012.

60. Cabrera N, LeMonda C. *Handbook of Father Involvement.* Routledge; 2013.

61. Feldman R, Rosenthal Z, Eidelman A. Maternal-preterm skin-to-skin contact enhances child physiological organization and cognitive control across first 10 years of life. *J Biol Psychiatry.* 2014;75:56–64.

62. Varela N, et al. Cortisol and blood pressure levels decrease in fathers during the first hour of skin-to-skin contact with their premature babies. *Acta Paediatr.* 2018; 107:628–632.

63. Shorey S, Hong-Gu H, Morelius E. Skin-to-skin contact by fathers and the impact on infant and paternal outcomes: An integrative review. *Midwifery.* 2016;40:207–217.

64. Hazen N, McFarland L, Jacobvitz D, Soisson E. Fathers' frightening behaviors and sensitivity with infants. In: Newland L, Freeman H, Coyl D, eds. *Emerging Topics in Father Attachment.* Routledge; 2011:50–69.

65. Paquette D, Bigras M. The risky situation. In: Newland L, Freeman H, Coyl D, eds. *Emerging Topics in Father Attachment.* Routledge; 2011:32–50.

66. Flinn M. Evolution and ontogeny of stress response to social challenges in the human child. *Dev Rev.* 2006;26:138–174.

67. Flinn M, Muehlenbein M, Ponzi D. Evolution of neuroendocrine mechanisms linking attachment and life history in middle childhood. *Behav Brain Sci.* 2009; 32:27–28.

68. Pendry P, Adam E. Association between parent's marital functioning and child cortisol levels. *Int J Behav Dev.* 2007;1:1–2.

69. Hollanders J, Van Der Voorn B, Rotteveel J, Finken M. Is HPA axis reactivity in childhood gender specific? A systematic review. *Biol Sex Differ.* 2017;11:1–11.

70. Nielsen L. *Father-Daughter Relationships: Contemporary Research and Issues.* Routledge, second edition; 2019.

71. Luecken L, Kraft A, Hagan M. Negative relationships in the family predict attenuated cortisol in emerging adults. *Horm Behav.* 2009;55:412–417.

72. Byrd J, Auer B, Grander D, Massey A. The father-daughter dance: Relationship quality and daughters' stress response. *J Fam Psychol.* 2012;26:87–94.

73. Johnson V, Gans S. Parent cortisol and family relatedness predict anxious behavior in emerging adults. *J Fam Psychol.* 2018;30:802–811.
74. Coley R, Bjarnason T, Carrano J. Does early paternal parenting promote low-income children's long-term cognitive skills? *J Fam Issues.* 2011;32:1522–1542.
75. Fagan J, Lee Y. Effects of fathers' and mothers' cognitive stimulation and income on toddlers' cognition. *Fathering.* 2014;10:140–158.
76. Pancsofar N, Feagans L. Fathers' early contributions to children's language development in families from low-income rural communities. *Early Child Res Q.* 2010; 25:450–463.
77. LeMonda C, McFadden K. Fathers from low-income backgrounds. In: Lamb M, ed. *Role of the Father in Child Development.* Wiley and Sons; 2010: 296–319.
78. McFadden K. Low-income father engagement in learning activities in early childhood. *Fam Sci.* 2012;2:120–130.
79. Sethna V, et al. Father-child interactions at 3 months and 24 months: Contributions to children's cognitive development at 24 months. *Infant Ment Health J.* 2017; 38:378–390.
80. Aldous J, Mulligan G. Father's child care and children's behavior problems. *J Fam Issues.* 2002;23:624–647.
81. Ramchandani P. Differential susceptibility to fathers' care and involvement: The moderating effect of infant reactivity. *Fam Sci.* 2010;1:93–101.
82. St George J, Wroe J, Cashin M. The concept and measurement of fathers' stimulating play: A review. *Attach Hum Dev.* 2018;20:634–658.
83. Boyce R, et al. Early father involvement and mental health problems in middle childhood. *Am J Child Adolesc Psychiatry.* 2006;45:1510–1523.
84. Sarkadi A, Kirstiansson R, Oberklai F, Bremberg S. Fathers' involvement and children's developmental outcomes. *Acta Paediatr.* 2008;97:153–158.
85. Leidy M, Schofield T, Parke R. Fathers' contributions to children's social development. In: Cabrera N, LeMonda C, eds. *Handbook of Father Involvement.* Routledge; 2013:151–168.
86. Grossman L, Grossman L, Kindler H, Zimmerman P. Attachment and exploration: The influences of parents on psychological security from infancy to adulthood. In: Cassidy J, Shaver P, eds. *Handbook of Attachment.* Guilford Press; 2008: 857–879.
87. Carothers B, Reis H. Men and women are from earth: Examining the latent structure of gender. *J Pers Soc Psychol.* 2012;104:385–407.
88. Balliet D, Li N, Macfarlan S, Van Vugt M. Sex differences in cooperation: A meta-analytic review of social dilemmas. *Psychol Bull.* 2011;137:881–909.
89. Eliot L. *Pink Brain Blue Brain.* Houghton Mifflin; 2009.
90. Maccoby E, Jacklin C. *The Psychology of Sex Differences.* Stanford University Press; 1974.
91. Walker L. Gender and morality. In: Killen M, Smetana J, eds. *Handbook of Moral Development.* Erlbaum; 2006:93–115.
92. Koestner R, Franz C, Winberger J. The family origins of empathic concern: A 26-year longitudinal study. *Personal Soc Psychol.* 1990;58:709–718.
93. Hashmi S, Vanderwert R, Price H, Gerson S. Exploring the benefits of doll play through neuroscience. *Front Hum Neurosci.* 2020; 14–22.

94. Cabrera N, Karberg E, Malin J, Aldoney D. The magic of play: Low-income mothers' and fathers' playfulness and children's emotional regulation and vocabulary skills. *Infant Ment Health J*. 2017;38:1–14.

95. Dockterman E. It can be a boy, a girl, neither or both. *Time*. Oct 7 2019. Published online 2019.

96. Frederick D. Mattel brings dads into the Barbie narrative. *PR Week*. 2017; April 14, 2017.

97. McLanahan S, Tach L, Schneider D. The causal effects of father absence. *Annu Rev Sociol*. 2013;22:399–427.

98. Yeung J, Duncan G, Hill M. Putting fathers back in the picture: Parental activities and children's adult outcomes. *Marriage Fam Rev*. 2008;29:97–113.

99. Ali S, Khaleque A, Rohner R. Pancultural gender differences in the relation between perceived parental acceptance and psychological adjustment of children and adult offspring: A meta-analytic review of worldwide research from 22 countries. *J Cross Cult Psychol*. 2015;46:1059–1080.

100. Carroll L. *Alice's Adventures in Wonderland*. MacMillan; 1920.

FATHERS AS PARENTING PARTNERS

SLOUCHES ON COUCHES AND OTHER NONSENSE

DOI: 10.4324/9781003324003-4

Our negative beliefs and damaging stereotypes about fathers range from the somewhat curious and confusing and to the downright silly and flat-out insulting. Many of those false beliefs are rooted in our idealized, overly flattering beliefs about mothers. So in this chapter, we will be uprooting some of our most popular myths about mothers.

Box 4.1 Are you fooling yourself? The biology of dads

Which of the following do you believe are true?

1. Men lack the instinct for parenting that women are born with.
2. Unlike fathers, mothers can interpret their babies' cries.
3. After their child is born, women's hormones change but men's do not.
4. Unlike men, women have a biological drive to become parents.
5. Unlike fathers, mothers instinctively know what their babies need.

MATERNAL INSTINCT: FATHERS ARE "INSTINCT" CHALLENGED, BLESS THEIR LITTLE HEARTS.

Let's begin at the beginning—the years before any man or woman becomes a parent. Most of us are probably exposed to the belief that men, by nature, lack an inborn instinct to want children or to know how to care for them as newborns, Box 4.1 illustrates. Women, by contrast, presumably have the big advantage—maternal instinct. Not having the maternal instinct app that "mother" nature installed in all females, men don't know how to take care of babies the way women do. Men are, as nature intended, behind in the parenting race from the get-go. Put more crassly, men are inferior to women as parents.

But here's the thing: There is no such thing as maternal instinct.[1] Then why do so many people believe it? Part of the problem is with the word "instinct." An instinct is not the same as a need, a desire, or a preference. An instinct is an inborn behavior that every member of that species or of that gender possesses. Instinctive behavior is automatic, not learned. Instincts do not come and go. For example, fear is instinctive. All human beings throughout history and throughout the world feel afraid when they encounter circumstances that they believe might hurt, injure, or kill them. And when we feel afraid, our bodies instinctively respond by releasing more cortisol and raising our heart rate and blood pressure. Instincts are universal. If there was a maternal instinct, it would be as strong in the 1800s or the 1950s as it is today and it would produce the same behaviors in all women throughout the world.

How do we know human females do not have a maternal instinct?[1] Let's start with the fact that young women are more likely than in the past to say they don't want to be mothers. Why? Largely because they are more educated and committed to careers. Leaving education aside, 10% of women choose not to have children—a number that jumps to 20% for women with undergraduate degrees and 33% for women with graduate or professional degrees.[2,3] Then too, young American men are just as likely as women to say they want to have children.[4] And 10% of mothers say they wavered and felt very ambivalent, sometimes for years, before making the leap into motherhood.[5] Moreover, almost one in ten mothers says she regrets having had children.[6] Women are just as likely as men to regret having had kids.[7]

What about the thousands of women who give up their babies soon after they are born? Nearly 3,500 women in the U.S. alone served as surrogates between 2000 and 2013.[8] And what about the 18,000 American mothers who give their babies up for adoption every year?[9] These mothers are giving up their baby at the very time when maternal instinct is supposed to be at highest pitch. What happened to their "instinct" to bond with and protect their child?

The belief in maternal instinct also falls flat in other ways. First-time mothers do not instinctively know how to take care of a baby—which is why they turn to the internet, books, relatives, and nannies for motherhood mentoring. Mothering skills are learned, not instinctive. And while learning these skills, first-time mothers often feel frustrated, overwhelmed, and disheartened. All of this, of course, can contribute to becoming clinically depressed in the first year of their baby's life.[10] This also helps explain why mothers are more likely than fathers to physically abuse and neglect their babies.[11] How does any of this square with the idea that women have an instinct that men lack for wanting children and for taking care of their newborns?

Even if maternal instinct is nothing more than an old wives' tale, what harm can it do? Quite a bit, as we can see. The myth feeds the false assumption that fathers are less competent and less attached to their baby. And too many new mothers feel guilty, ashamed, and depressed because they can't live up to the maternal instinct myth. If either parent believes women have an instinct for parenting that men lack, the dad is likely to feel less confident, less competent, and less necessary. Instead of stepping up or taking the lead in taking care of their baby, he is apt to step back. And his stepping back reinforces the stereotype that men don't know how to take care of babies and aren't deeply attached to their newborns. The myth benefits no one—not the mom, or the dad or the baby. The mom needs a full-fledged parenting partner, not a self-doubting sidekick. And the baby needs a fully engaged, confident father. In short, the myth of maternal instinct is not a harmless.

THE HORMONE DISADVANTAGE: FATHERS FALL SHORT AGAIN?

Hand in hand with the myth of maternal instinct is the notion that men do not undergo any hormonal changes like women do when they become fathers. And this, in turn, further handicaps the dad because these hormonal changes lead to better parenting skills and stronger bonding with the baby. Do all these hormonal advantages go solely to the biological mother? And if that's the case, then what does this mean for all the millions of women who adopt a baby or have their baby through a surrogate, since none of those mothers undergo the hormonal changes of pregnancy?

Are dads "hormone handicapped," so to speak? No, they are not. We now know that fathers undergo similar hormonal changes to biological mothers—and these changes begin before the baby is born.[12,13] As is true for mothers, fathers' hormonal changes lead to greater synchrony with their baby. Synchrony is the parent's ability to be attuned to the baby's emotions and social signals. And being more attuned or in sync with their baby, the parent communicates with and senses the baby's needs more easily. As we will see, as fathers and babies strengthen this synchrony by interacting with each other, they are having an impact on each other's hormone levels, making them more alike biologically—a desirable situation referred to as bio-synchrony.

Like women, men also experience an increase in oxytocin during the pregnancy and after the baby's birth. Oxytocin, commonly referred to as the "love" hormone, is linked to being more engaged, more affectionate, and more strongly bonded to another person. This phenomenon of love at first sight is reported by both mothers and fathers (sometimes more sheepishly by fathers). Interestingly, couples who live together during pregnancy have more similar levels of oxytocin than couples who live apart. For fathers and for mothers, the increased oxytocin means being more focused, more affectionate, and more engaged with their baby. The powerful role that oxytocin plays in bonding to our babies is highlighted in one particularly distinctive study. Researchers sprayed oxytocin or a placebo into fathers' noses. Then they watched how the dads played with their five-month-old babies. The oxytocin-boosted fathers played more energetically and were more attuned to their babies. More fascinating still, the babies' oxytocin increased after playing with their boosted dads. Oxytocin is nothing to sneeze at, so to speak.[14]

Men's cortisol levels also rise, as do women's, when they become parents. The adrenal gland releases more cortisol when we are stressed. This cortisol boost gives us more physical energy and lowers our sensitivity to pain. These cortisol gifts help us cope better and react faster when we're faced with risky, intimidating, stressful, or downright dangerous situations. It's the "how did I lift that 3,000 pound car off my baby?" hormone. Because parenting is stressful, especially for first-time parents, both fathers and mothers have higher levels of cortisol than adults without children. These first-time moms and dads with four to six-month-old babies had higher levels of stress hormones and also higher levels of the "feel good" and bonding hormones—endorphin and oxytocin.[15]

A man's testosterone levels also change as he is becoming a father.[16] When a man is living with a pregnant woman or with a newborn child, his testosterone levels decrease, never rising again to the level they were before he became a father. Lower levels of testosterone are linked to less aggression, more empathy, and more activity in the area of the brain that processes emotions. Men with lower testosterone levels are also more responsive to a baby's cries. Indeed, the more experience a man or a woman has had taking care of infants before their child is born, the greater their hormonal changes are after their baby is born.

But our hormones are not stagnant. They fluctuate based on the kinds of situations we find ourselves in and how we behave in those situations. Our behavior and our hormones are interwoven in a looping cycle. Changes in one contribute to changes in the other. For example, when he is being affectionate or playing with his baby, the dad's oxytocin increases. And as his oxytocin increases, he becomes even more playful and engaged which further increases his oxytocin. This looping between hormones and behavior holds true for both mothers and fathers in respect to their babies. For example, when a father holds his premature baby against his bare chest, his prolactin increases while his testosterone, blood pressure, and heart rate decrease.[17] This, in turn, allows him to be more attuned to the baby. Again biosynchrony is taking place. He and his baby become more physically relaxed as their stress hormones fall. Similarly, when a father hears his baby cry, his testosterone level rises. If he is allowed to go to comfort his child, his testosterone level falls. But if he is not allowed to comfort his baby, his testosterone level remains high.[12] Our bodies have been doing this for millennia, even though modern science has only recently allowed us to measure what is going on. Mother Nature and Father Time have worked well together creating this synchronicity between our hormones and our behavior.

In sum, men as well as women reap the benefits of hormonal changes when they become parents. Of course, the greatest hormonal changes take place in pregnant and nursing mothers. But fathers, as well as adoptive mothers, also get a hormone boost that contributes to bonding, communicating, nurturing, and being in sync with their babies.

BLUE BRAIN, PINK BRAIN: DAD'S INFERIOR BRAIN

Hand in hand with the notion that men are inferior when it comes to instincts and hormones is the idea that men's brains are more poorly "wired" than women's for the tasks involved in parenting a young child. That is, men's brains are hard-wired to lose the contest with women when it comes to nurturing, bonding, understanding, or communicating with their babies. Dad has a blockhead brain in comparison to mom's blockbuster brain. Fortunately, thanks to the development of brain scans, researchers have been able to debunk this myth head-on, so to speak. As it turns out, dads' brains, just like moms' brains, undergo changes after their baby is born—changes that contribute to stronger bonds, increased engagement, and greater attentiveness and nurturing.[18]

When parents hear their baby cry or look at pictures of their baby, similar areas of the brain become activated in mothers and in fathers—or in father and father or mother and mother families, for that matter. While watching a video of their baby playing, those areas of the brain linked to interpreting social cues and being empathetic became more active. In the first four months of their babies' lives, dads' brains are changing in ways that parallel the changes in mothers' brains—changes that occur in those areas of the brain that affect bonding, empathy, and responsiveness to other people.[19]

An intriguing study with gay and heterosexual fathers clearly illustrates how the brain, hormones and behavior are intertwined.[20] When two gay fathers were raising their five-month-old baby, the father who spent the most time with the baby had higher oxytocin levels and more brain activity in the area linked to bonding and nurturing. The same was true to mothers in heterosexual marriages where the moms were doing most of the child-care. It was not the parents' gender or sexual orientation that affected their brains and hormones. And regardless of which parent was providing most of the care, oxytocin and brain activity increased for all parents when they were interacting with their baby.

This is not to deny that mothers undergo greater hormonal changes during pregnancy and while breastfeeding than fathers or mothers who adopt babies or have babies through surrogacy. But regardless of their gender, sexual orientation, or biological connection to the baby, parents' brains become more activated in those areas that help them bond and nurture their child. In short, brain scans and blood tests show that fathers do have baby-oriented brains and baby friendly hormones just as mothers do, even when those mothers did not give birth to the child.

BABY BONDS AND ATTACHMENT: MOM WINS

Box 4.2. Are you fooling yourself? What babies want and need?

Which of these do you think are true?

1. Newborns form an immediate emotional bond with their mothers.
2. Toddlers are as emotionally attached to their fathers as to their mothers.
3. Babies consider their mothers to be more important than any other person.
4. When very young babies are separated from their mothers, they become upset.
5. Young babies are usually afraid of strangers.
6. Babies form the strongest bond with the parent who spends the most time with them.
7. Babies and toddlers go to their mothers for comfort, not to their fathers.
8. Babies who spend too much time in daycare become less attached to their moms.
9. Babies recognize their mother's face and voice before they recognize their fathers'.
10. Babies rated as insecurely attached have weak, troubled relationships with their parents.

Still, isn't it true that babies quickly and automatically form a primary attachment to their mother—an attachment that surpasses their bonds to their father? And isn't the baby's attachment to the dad far less important and far less beneficial—especially in the first year or so of their baby's life? From the baby's perspective, isn't dad pretty much just a sideshow, while mom is the main event? And doesn't this all-powerful, all-consuming attachment to the mother become weaker if she spends too much time away from the baby? Consider the popular beliefs in Box 4.2.

As popular as these beliefs might be, they melt away under the weight of the scientific evidence.[21–24] Most parents probably won't like this news: Babies are biologically programmed to engage with and be responsive to *any* and *all* adults who regularly provide care for them—nannies, grannies, and daycare workers. It doesn't much matter to the baby. Another fact parents might not want to hear—especially at 3 AM when they're trying to soothe their wailing infant—is that in the first seven months or so, babies are not capable of forming emotional attachments to anyone—not to mom, or dad, or doting grandparents. Yes, babies vocalize, smile, and wriggle around joyfully with the adults in their lives. To the caregiving, loving parent, the baby's behavior is a sure sign that "my baby loves me." At the risk of breaking some hearts here, that is not what is happening. Before six to seven months of age, babies are not capable of forming an emotional attachment to anyone. We adults are interchangeable sources of entertainment and caregiving. This is why babies don't become stressed or afraid when one caregiver hands them over to another caregiver or when neither of their parents are around. Babies have no fear of strangers because everyone is, in effect, a stranger—including their parents. In fact, babies can't even recognize people's faces. But between seven and nine months, things change. Babies start to recognize faces, to tell the difference between their parents and other adults, to be wary of strangers, and to develop emotional attachments. But here's the biggest news: The baby forms *equally* strong attachments to mom and to dad—or in the case of lesbian and gay couples, to both of their moms and both of their dads. To the baby, dad is just as primary, as important, and as necessary as mom. There is no hierarchy with one primary and one secondary parent.[24]

Yes, but since most mothers spend far more time than fathers do with their babies, doesn't that mean the baby is more bonded to her? No, it does not. A baby is not more bonded or attached to the parent who provides the most care.[25] Of course, a parent has to provide enough consistent care for the baby to perceive that person as a caregiver. But babies do not keep track of parenting hours and dole out their love and affection accordingly. One of the world's leading experts on early childhood attachment, Everett Waters, puts it even more bluntly.[28]

"The word *attachment* distracts you from seeing what you are talking about. Some think that doubling up on parent time could get you even more attachment, a higher dose so to speak. That causes you to ask the wrong questions and frame the wrong answers. It is important to realize that attachment development runs the entire lifespan. Otherwise you think infancy is the period of inoculation, so that if the job is done then, well there, it guarantees certain outcomes in the future. That is not the case. There is no way of measuring the strength of attachment. The less often we use the word attachment, the better off we'll all be."

(pp. 475–476)

Especially back in the 1950s, people often fell for the attachment myths—myths that sidelined fathers and glorified mothers. But the glorification came at a price. The mother-infant bond was supposedly so important that mothers should not spend much time apart from their babies because it would weaken their bond. And if that happened, those babies would develop emotional, behavioral, and relationship problems later in life. This myth put tremendous pressure on employed parents who had to leave their babies in daycare while they both worked. It is no coincidence that this notion became popular when men were returning from World War II and needed their jobs back—jobs that women had been performing throughout the war. What better way to convince women to be happy about going back to being housewives than to scare the wits out of them with the mother-infant attachment myths? The myths finally bit the dust, but only after researchers had conducted hundreds of studies on children in daycare centers. The result? The children who were in daycare, even up to 35 hours a week, had no weaker attachments to their mothers and developed no more emotional or behavioral problems than children who had not been in daycare.[26,27]

This is not to say that babies get along just fine when they are separated from both parents for long periods of time. They are not fine. Between 7 and 24 months of age, babies are really stressed out, physically and emotionally, when they are separated from both parents for even a few days. Once researchers realized this, hospitals changed their policies and placed fewer restrictions on parents staying with their hospitalized children.[25]

Another attachment myth is that researchers can measure how attached a child is to each parent. In other words, there is a "scientific" way of finding out whether dad is more important or has a better relationship with the child than mom does. For that matter, it would be a way to finding out whether any particular parent has a better relationship with their child than some other parent. That would be a helpful test, now wouldn't it? Except, there is no such test. What confuses people is that there are tests called "attachment" tests—which is a very misleading name because these tests do not measure the kind of relationship, attachment, or bond a child has with the parent.[28]

And the tests certainly can't tell us which parent is more important or closer to the child. Put in the very simplest terms, these are "stress" tests to see how a very young child reacts toward their parent when they are placed in a stressful or extremely challenging situation—not how the child behaves in their normal day-to-day interactions with their parents. When under stress, the child who comfortably goes to the parent for reassurance and comfort is classified as having a secure attachment style. And the child who avoids or ignores the parent or who seems confused or angry about asking for comfort is classified as having an insecure attachment style. These tests have nothing to do with the parents' relationship with the child. And this is why some children who behave in an insecure way during the stress test have very secure, loving relationships with their parents, while children who behave in a secure way on the test sometimes have an unhealthy or even an abusive relationship with their parents.[29]

Here are the three take-away messages about babies' attachments to their fathers. First, the young child's emotional bond to dad is just as strong and just as important as the bond to mom. Second, this is true even though most dads are not able to spend nearly as much time with their babies as moms spend. Third, babies form a bond with dad and mom at about the same point in time, around seven months of age. In short, we need to put those baby attachment myths to rest.

CHILDCARE WARS: LAZY, LOAFING DADS

Speaking of attachments, isn't it true that most fathers are not at all attached to the idea of doing their fair share of the childcare or work in the home? In fact, aren't most dads shirking their childcare and household responsibilities? And isn't this why we have so many jokes and books about lazy dads? Take this joke for example: The dad complains to his co-worker: "I'm so busy at home that I need three hands—one for the beer, one for the chips, and one for the TV remote." Or take a book like *All the Rage: Mothers, Fathers, and the Myth of Equal Partnership,* which soared to the top of the bestseller list in 2019 after it was released on Mother's Day. Lockman failed to include the major findings from recent research on gender equity at work and at home and grossly misrepresented findings even in the few studies she had selected to support her personal opinions, Box 4.3 illustrates. Despite this, her book zoomed to the bestseller list, as too often happens when a book reinforces popular stereotypes that are extremely flattering to one group—the victims—while demonizing another group—the bullies.

Box 4.3 Throw the book at him: Dad bashing books

On Mother's Day in 2019, *All the rage: Mothers, fathers and the myth of equal partnership* was released to great acclaim in many of the most prestigious newspapers across the country.[30] The author, Darcy Lockman, is a career journalist who later became a therapist. Based largely on interviews with 50 mothers and a handful of social scientists, Lockman claims that most husbands are lazy, selfish, and sexist. They knowingly and intentionally exploit their wives, refusing to "appreciate the complexities of motherhood." Supposedly, the unfair division of labor in the home is "one of the most important gender equity issues of our time," leaving almost all mothers enraged. Among her many claims are that America is a society that "subdues women into submission," teaches girls and women to "keep their mouths shut," allows "male employees sit back while female workers perform tasks that don't lead to promotion," and reminds women "*daily*" that "it is our job to make men feel good."

Books and jokes that demean fathers are rooted in a deeply entrenched belief: Most husbands are slackers who shirk their childcare and household responsibilities. Before we dismantle this myth, take a minute to consider your current beliefs by taking the quiz in Box 4.4.

When it comes to how much childcare and housework mothers and fathers are doing, keep this adage in mind: "When people judge themselves, the verdict is always in their favor." Indeed, researchers have found that moms and dads over-estimate how much housework and childcare they do.[31,32]

Box 4.4 Fooling yourself? Men, housework, and childcare

Which of the following do you think are true?

Most American men ....

1. spend half as much time with their kids as the mothers do
2. only spend about three hours a week on chores at home
3. wish they could spend less time at work and more time with their kids
4. are less stressed than their wives trying to balance family and work
5. spend more time at work than their wives even when they have full-time jobs

Why does this matter? Because almost all research on the hours parents spend on housework and childcare comes from mothers' reports, not from fathers' reports. We know that mothers do more housework and childcare than fathers.[31,32] That is not the issue. The issue is how *much* more are women doing—more important still, is the overall workload for moms and dads different? Why does that matter? Because it feeds many of our negative assumptions about fathers.

Now back to the question: Are most mothers getting ripped off when it comes to the time that husbands and wives put into doing all that needs to be done to raise their children? No, they are not. According to national data from the Bureau of Labor Statistics and the American Time Use Surveys based on large national samples, the majority of mothers and fathers are equally sharing the workload. When paid and unpaid work are added together, both parents are spending about 62 hours a week doing what needs to be done to raise their children.[33,34] Let's replay that message: *There is no gender gap in the overall workload.*

Does this mean most couples are sharing the day-to-day, hands-on childcare and housework 50/50? No, it does not.[35] Especially when children are under the age of five, most couples decide the mother will do 65% of the direct childcare and work that needs to be done at home. And the father will do 65% of the financial childcare that gets done out of the home. Until the children reach school age, 30% of mothers work full time, 30% part time, and 40% don't work at all. As children get older, 75% of their moms are working, as are 90% of dads. Yes, dads are only spending 8 hours during the week with their kids, compared to 14 hours for moms. Why? Because dads have to spend so much more time away from home doing the "financial" childcare by earning most, or all, of the family's money.[36]

Let's peel pack the layers of the lazy father myths. In families where the mothers work outside the home, even when she only has a part-time job, each parent spends almost equal time with the kids. In fact, most employed mothers only spend about 30 minutes more a day with the children than their husbands do.[37] That's a pretty small difference especially since mothers who work full time generally spend 7 to 10 hours less than their husbands do.[35] This is because jobs that are classified as "full-time" range from as few as 35 hours to more than 70 hours a week. And most women are not in the most time-consuming jobs. For example, from 1979 through 2009, women and men who worked 50 hours a week earned the same salaries.[38] But only 3% of women compared to 20% of men worked at those demanding 50-hour jobs.[39] In fact, nearly 40% of men in professional jobs and 25% of men in middle-income jobs work at least 50 hours or more a week.[40]

Not only do husbands spend more time at work than their employed wives but the men's jobs are far less family friendly.[3] Men do most of the nightshift and early morning jobs—the jobs that cut most deeply into parenting time. In fact, two-thirds of workers who have to be at work before 8 AM are men.[51] And even when men and women are doing the same job, women are less willing to work on weekends and holidays or to work overtime, even though the pay is higher at those times. For example, in Boston from 2011 through 2017, women bus and train operators earned 11% less than the men. Why? Because the men worked 83% more weekend, holiday and overtime hours and took half as many unpaid days off work as the women.[41]

Men also have less time to spend with their children because they spend more time than women do commuting—which, in major metropolitan areas, can add as much as 7 to 14 hours to a person's workweek.[42] Women often have shorter commutes in part because they usually have more freedom than men to accept the lower-paying jobs that are more conveniently located close to home. In contrast, men are under more pressure to take jobs further from home because those jobs often pay more.

The belief that most fathers are lazy shirkers also runs off the rails on another level: Many couples do not *want* to share housework and childcare equally. If their family didn't need the money, 40% of mothers say they would stay home full time and 50% would only work part-time.[43] Most American men and women believe mothers should not work or should only work part-time until all the children are in school.[44] When 16,000 high school students were asked what they hoped for in their future families, most wanted the dad to work full time and the mom to stay home—and more of them felt this way in 2019 than their counterparts in 2015.[45]

Is this a sign that gender equity has stalled—and that men are to blame? How does that idea fly with the millions of American fathers and mothers who like their traditional gender division of labor in raising their children? Thud. Step back and consider, for example, the differences between college-educated and less-educated women's priorities and options. College-educated mothers generally find their jobs more enjoyable and more meaningful and get longer maternity leaves than less educated mothers.[46] Sharing the childcare and income earning 50/50 is a more appealing and more viable option for them. But to sneer at couples who don't share their roles anywhere nearly equally, to assume this proves that "gender equity has stalled," and to blame this traditional arrangement on men is not only insensitive, it's condescending. One size does not fit all. So maybe we need a "stop the sneer" slogan?

Books like *Ambitious Like a Mother: Why Prioritizing Your Career Is Good For Your Kids* are attention-grabbing.[47] But the reality is that men still carry most, or all, of the financial childcare burden. The soul-sucking, health-destroying work that so many fathers do robs them of what they say they want most: more time with their children. As one team of experts who have studied parents' workloads for decades discovered more than ten years ago: we are barking up the wrong tree when we keep insisting that sexism or laziness are the reasons men do less of the direct childcare and housework.[31,33]

Are mothers slackers because most of them are not carrying an equal load of the financial childcare? No. Are most dads shirking their childcare responsibilities, heading off to work every day cheerfully singing, "hi ho, hi ho, It's off to work I go?" No. Are some fathers and mothers failing to carry their fair share of the workload? You bet. But this doesn't change the fact that the vast majority of fathers and mothers are pulling their weight *equally* in doing what needs to be done to raise their children. For mothers and fathers, there are tradeoffs. You can't have it both ways, even though that's the way most of us want it. Which parent is getting the better deal? You decide.

CHORE WARS: DADS ARE SLOUCHES ON COUCHES

Box 4.5 Fooling yourself? Are dads slouches?

Which of these are true for most American families?

1. Dads spend half as much time as moms do with their kids.
2. The total hours of paid and unpaid work are about equal for mothers and fathers.
3. Wives spend about three times as much time on housework as their husbands.
4. Nearly all wives want to split childcare and income earning 50/50 with their husbands.
5. Most Americans believe mothers and fathers should spend equal time with the kids.

Have you heard the joke about the husband who griped to his wife: "You made me dust the furniture last week. So I did it. But now it's back. I won't let you trick me into that again." Or how about the husband whose idea of helping with housework is lifting his legs off the floor so his wife can vacuum? The slouches on couches messages are also promoted in books, for example: *The Lazy Husband: How to Get Men to Do More Parenting and Housework*[48] and *How Not to Hate Your Husband After Having Kids*,[49] Take a minute to explore your own beliefs by answering the questions in Box 4.5.

Are mothers losing the dust bunny, chore wars—and are their husbands the villains? Let's start with the majority of families—families where both parents are employed. How much more of the housework do you think these mothers do each week? 15 hours? 10? The answer is 3. Most wives do 15 hours of work in the home and husbands do 12.[50] Keep in mind though that not all these women have full-time jobs. When the mom has a part-time job, she puts in about four hours a day on childcare, housework, and cooking.[51] Of course, mothers who are not employed will spend more than four hours a day on those activities since their husbands are doing 100% of the financial children. But since the majority of moms are employed, they do ten hours less work at home than mothers did 25 years ago.[52]

Getting all riled up about women doing most of the housework and then blaming their husbands sweeps a lot of important facts under the rug. Let's first focus on two simple facts about women: Single women do about four more hours of housework a week than single men.[52] As for stay-at-home moms, college-educated women spend less time on housework and more time with their kids than less-educated mothers.[51] Then there's the age factor. Men and women aged 23 to 38 spend less time on housework, yard work, and cooking and more time taking care of their pets than 38- to 50-year-olds.[53] Clearly something is going on here other than a gender battle about household chores.

Actually, researchers have put one of these ideas to the test. Nearly 650 adults were shown pictures of a man or a woman sitting in either a clean or a messy room. Then they were asked how messy or clean the room was and how urgent it was to clean it up. Men and women had the same standards when it came to seeing the room as either messy or clean. But men *and women* were more likely to say the room needed to be cleaned up when the occupant was a woman. And in the messy room scenario, men and women judged the man as more irresponsible and lazier than the woman. The researchers concluded that they all fell for the stereotype that men are lazier and messier than women.[54]

Then there's another wrinkle: Men's contributions around the home are more invisible and less likely to get noticed or credited.[55,56] The work mothers usually do is hard to overlook: cooking, cleaning, vacuuming, and doing laundry. These jobs are also done on a regular basis. In contrast, dad's work

is more invisible and less routine: yard work, car and equipment mainte-
nance, cleaning gutters, resolving computer problems, repairing or assem-
bling things. For example, in a 2019 national Gallup poll, two-thirds of the
couples said the husband does most of the yard and car work and the wife
does most of the laundry and cooking.[55] As for which chores rack up the most
points in the housework contest and get the most applause, cooking probably
tops the list—the chore that is almost always done by mom.[57] Think about
it. How often do dads get noticed, let alone thanked, for changing the oil in
the car or cleaning the gutters?

Here's the point: The main reason most husbands do less of the work in
and around the home is the same reason they don't get to spend as much time
with the children as their wives: their jobs. We might grouse and grumble
about this. But that doesn't justify villainizing men as lazy bums who do
nothing more than lift their legs off the floor so their wives can vacuum.

THE PARENTING LOAD: DAD'S FREELOAD. MOMS OVERLOAD.

Who gets the shorter end of the parenting workload stick—mom or dad?
If we trust the stereotypes, we know the answer: Mom gets the short end.
And who is largely to blame for that? Stereotype answer: dads. Now let's
step back and remember that we are approaching this like detectives, not
like stereotype slaves. We have downloaded the CRAAP test as well as an
app for "how to dupe dopes." We start by looking for evidence at the scene
of the crime—a crime where mom is assumed to be the victim and dad is
presumably our main suspect.

By carefully following the clues and then connecting the dots, here's what
we discover. Compared to the 22 other richest countries, the U.S. is dead
last in providing free or low-cost, subsidized childcare and in providing paid
maternity and paternity leaves.[58] Americans get fewer paid vacations and fewer
unemployment, disability, and retirement benefits than people in other rich
countries.[59] This, in turn, puts greater pressure on American men to maximize their incomes which means spending less time at home. Nordic countries have the most father-friendly, family-friendly policies in the world. And
Nordic dads do more childcare and housework than dads anywhere else on
the planet.[60] Are some of our national policies accomplices to the "crime"?

And now another clue: The cost of taking time off work to take care of
young children. Let's start with the most highly educated Americans. Take
the example of Harvard graduates who took 18 months off work early in
their careers. Fifteen years later, they were still paying a price compared to
those who had never taken time off. The MBAs who took time off were
earning 40% less, PHDs 30% less, and MDs 15% less.[61] Now consider this
hypothetical of a less educated American, 26-year-old Abe who earns

$44,000. His wife keeps working because she earns more. Given the cost of daycare, Abe takes five years off to stay home until both kids are in school, at a loss of $220,000. Then Abe goes back to work. Decades later, when Abe retires, those five years off have cost him $706,778. Why? Because Abe lost five years of retirement benefits with accumulating interest over those decades and lost five years of salary increases.[62]

The deeper we dig, the closer we get to finding our villain. Only one-third of wives earn more than their husbands.[63] Given the high costs of daycare, 40% of employed moms have to quit work and another 40% have to cut back their hours. Meanwhile, 75% of their husbands have to keep working full time—often having to spend more time at work to make up for the wife's lost income.[64] The higher the husband's income, the more likely it is his wife will quit working after they have kids.[3] Lucky for us, another detective has joined us: Claudia Goldin, a world-famous economics professor at Harvard who has spent decades researching gender differences in the workforce and home.[3] Here's her big find: The choices that women make in their jobs long before they have children have a major impact on which parent eventually ends up doing more of the childcare and housework.

Now our detective work gets more intense and we ask: What choices have most women made that could in any way contribute to this "crime?" Even though more women (45%) than men (35%) under the age of thirty have a college degree, women still choose to enter the lower paying, more family friendly fields.[64] For instance, in 2019, women earned 65% of undergraduate and Master's Degrees and a little over 50% of Doctorates. But as Box 4.6 shows us, most women choose fields that are more family friendly even though the pay is lower.[3]

But here's the paycheck punchline: It's *not* the type of job or the field she chose that has the biggest impact on a woman's income. It's the choices she makes once she is in that job. Women earn about 80% of what men earn.

Box 4.6 Undergraduate degrees in 2019*[65]

	Male	Female
Business	208,000	183,000
Computer science	70,000	18,000
Engineering	114,000	31,000
Mathematics	13,000	10,000
Psychology	24,000	92,000s
Education	15,000	69,000
Health professions	39,000	211,000

* Rounded to nearest thousand

But that is *not* because they get paid less than men for doing the same work—and *not* because there is widespread sex discrimination in the workforce. Yes, there are cases where a woman is getting paid less for equal work—and where sexism has hurt her financially. But this is not true for the vast majority of women, based on complicated statistical analyses of recent national data.[3]

Once a person has landed a job, what choices have the biggest impact on their income?[3] Regardless of the type of job, "how to make the most money" rules are basically the same: work longer hours, take jobs with the least flexible schedules, do more overtime, holiday, and on-call work, and do more work that requires in-person time with clients, difficult decision-making that affects many other people, and intense competition. Connect the dots: jobs that pay less = more time to spend at home with the kids = doing more of the work in the home = having a spouse who does most of the income earning = being able to take the job that pays less in the first place.

Remember that we already have an alleged villain in mind: Husbands. Let's see if we're on the right trail by applying national data to Jack and Jill—a married couple where the wife does more of the childcare and housework than the husband. Jack and Jill get married after they both graduate from law school. Before having kids, they both work 45 hours a week and earn the same income. Flash forward 15 years. They have two kids. Jill gave up practicing law to work in the private sector, where she doesn't have to work 45 hours a week and, of course, earns far less than Jack. Can you see why Jill is the one who has done more of the childcare and housework over the years? This example is based on actual research. Male and female lawyers who are specializing in the same field make the same incomes when they graduate. But fifteen years later, only 55% of female lawyers work 45 hours a week, in contrast to 80% of male lawyers. Female lawyers also quit practicing law to take lower-paying, private-sector jobs far more often than male lawyers. And male and female lawyers who continue working at least 45 hours a week after they graduate from law school make similar incomes.[3]

Here are a few other examples of Jack and Jill choices that have a major impact on how couples divvy up the paid and unpaid work after they have kids.[3] Male doctors work ten more hours a week than female doctors even when they are in the same field. Most women choose specialties that pay less because they work fewer hours and have more flexible schedules. For example, 60% of dermatologists and 75% of obstetricians and gynecologists are women. Even then, one-third of female pediatricians only work part-time. In contrast, 90% of orthopedic surgeons and 80% of cardiovascular disease doctors are men. And women are less likely than men to take on the burden of starting their own practice, even though the pay is higher.

As detectives on this case, we're also beginning to have doubts about the motives of our presumed villains—the husbands. There's got to be something in it for villains since there's always a chance they will get caught. So the following discoveries are throwing us off in terms of motives: In 25 countries, the higher the percentage of women who work outside the home, the higher the percentage of men who do housework and childcare, *regardless of how liberal or conservative their country's gender roles are.*[66] Then too, people who work more than 50 hours a week—instead of taking jobs that would let them stay home to do more childcare and housework—are more likely to have heart problems, strokes, high blood pressure, insomnia, job injuries, and to smoke, drink and use drugs.[67] And the vast majority of people doing those soul-sucking, health-destroying jobs are men.[67] Instead of taking safer, lower-paying jobs, why are many men doing work that is literally killing them—with 387 women and 4,803 men dying from work-related injuries in 2016 alone?[52] These work-related health problems also help to explain why, on average, American men die five years before women.[68] And the least educated dads with the lowest paying jobs are the most dissatisfied with how little time they get to spend with their children.[69] Worldwide, nearly 65% of fathers in a recent study in 20 countries wanted to share the parenting time equally. But only one-third of them were able to share equally because of the demands of their work.[40]

Now, as detectives on the housework/childcare crime scene, what have we decided? Who are the villains and who are the victims? Who or what else might we see as accomplices? And if our society or individual couples want to reduce the incidents of this particular "crime," what needs to be done? That is the question that will be answered in the final chapter of this book. For now, the case closed.

FAMILY-WORK STRESS: DAD'S "LESS STRESS" PASS

Box 4.7 The cost of raising a child[70]

$230,000–$270,000—not including college
29% housing
16% childcare & education (not including college)
18% food
15% transportation
 7% miscellaneous
 9% health care
 6% clothes

Even if we admit that fathers are not the "bad guys" in the childcare/house-work dilemmas that most couples face, isn't it still true that men are getting a "less stress pass" when it comes to balancing family and work? Aren't employed mothers more stressed out than their husbands?

Let's unpack this multi-layered bag. Most fathers wish they could spend less time at work and more time with their kids. And less educated men are just as likely as college-educated men to feel this way. Many, if not most, dads feel that even though society pays lip service to the importance of work-life balance and fathering time, we don't really mean it. And they have good reason to think so. Most Americans still think the dad should be the main, or the sole, financial provider for the family.[63] The pressure to maximize their income often leads to longer work hours, more commuting, more overtime and holiday work, more dangerous jobs, and less down time at home, including time with their kids. Even when their wives have full-time jobs, men spend 7 to 10 hours more at work every week, more time commuting, work more overtime and holiday hours, and have less flexible schedules. And as we've just seen, men's jobs take a bigger toll than women's jobs in terms of their physical health.

Since dads usually shoulder most—or all—of the responsibility for earning the family's money, they are apt to be especially stressed by the high costs of raising a child.[70] For a child born in 2020, parents will shell out about $270,000, which does *not* include the cost of a college education. As Box 4.7 shows, housing accounts for about a third of the total cost, followed by childcare. Of course, the costs vary dramatically based on where the family lives, with the Northeast being the most expensive. Back in 2015, families with a total income of more than $107,000 spent $20,000–$23,000 a year per child, compared to only $10,000 for families earning less than $60,000. And the costs go up as the child grows up, with teenagers being the most expensive. As one female Princeton sociologist put it, "children are economically worthless, but emotionally priceless."[71]

If he is the main wage earner, the father might also be more stressed than his wife because he sees what lies ahead financially. There are the staggering costs of college education and high price tags for his children's future weddings. Maybe it even crosses his mind that, at some future point, he's going to need enough money to pay for his parents' funerals, with an average price tag of $9,000.[72] Then there are the financial strains when "failure to launch" or "boomerang" adult children move back home—with only half of them chipping in anything for food or rent.[73] If this seems like nitpicking, get this: This is the first time since 2015 that young adults are more likely to still be living with their parents than with a romantic partner. And many of them are struggling with mental health, drinking, or drug problems.[74] Is it any wonder that these parents are more clinically depressed than parents whose adult children are financially self-reliant?[75] In part because they have given or "loaned" so much money to their adult children, parents in their sixties are three times as likely to file for bankruptcy as their counterparts in 1990.[76] Remember too that, compared to parents in other rich countries, many Americans are stressing themselves out financially and emotionally by going overboard in parenting—too much coddling, pampering, and unnecessary "rescuing."[77]

Are fathers getting a stress-free pass when it comes to balancing work and family? No, they are not. Fathers have as much, and often more, work-family stress than their employed wives, especially dads who work more than 50 hours a week.[40,63,78] More disturbing still, when parents feel burned out trying to balance the demands of work and family, fathers are more prone than mothers to suicidal thinking.[79] Of course there are employed mothers who are stressed out and burned out. And some of them have jobs that are far more demanding and stressful than their husbands' jobs. Still, the notion that mothers are far more stressed out than fathers is far off the mark.

PARENTHOOD: DADS CARE LESS

Even though most men spend less time with their children because of the demands of their jobs, isn't it still true that men generally don't enjoy parenting as much as women do? Aren't women still much more emotionally committed than men are to their children? Before exploring what the research has to say about this, try conducting another research study on your own. Using the questions in Box 4.8, interview a dozen fathers, including your own. See how their answers stack up with the research.

Box 4.8 Ask a man: Feelings about fatherhood

1. What have you enjoyed most and least about being a dad?
2. How has being a father changed you?
3. As a young father, what worried you most?
4. What do you wish you had known before having kids?
5. What are your greatest strengths and weaknesses as a dad?
6. How did your relationship with your dad influence the kind of dad you are?
7. How have your ideas and your behavior as a father changed over time?
8. What is the best gift or compliment your children have given you?
9. How has your relationship with each of your kids changed over the years?
10. What do you wish you had done or could do differently as a dad?
11. What do you wish your children had known or could know about you as a dad?
12. What do you wish you had more of and less of in your family life?
13. What holds you back, or held you back, from being a better dad?
14. What are you most worried about for each of your children?
15. What do you hope your children will say about you as a parent after you die?

Let's face up to the bad news: Sometimes parenting is a grind, a bore, and a burden. Even though having children comes with unrivaled times of joy, it also comes with unrivaled times of boredom, frustration, exhaustion, disappointment, and heartbreak. As the old saying goes, "you can't have your cake and eat it too." One female psychologist put it more bluntly: "Children are a huge source of joy, but they turn every other source of joy to shit."[80] Both men and women say that marital happiness goes down and stress goes up after they have children—a well-documented fact from almost 100 studies stretching back to the 70s.[80] For instance, in a survey of 1,500 parents nearly a third of them said that having children fell short of their expectations.[81] In some large surveys, fathers and employed mothers say that, on a day-to-day basis, their job is usually more rewarding and more fun than parenting.[82] This doesn't mean most parents don't love their children. It means that the day in day out work of parenting isn't usually the most enjoyable or meaningful part of the day. For example, in surveys with more than 14,000 parents, most marriages got happier after the kids were raised and gone.[83] And even though most parents do not regret having had children, both fathers and mothers often regret the sacrifices they have had to make.[84] Part of the yuck factor, of course, is the financial strain that children put on parents, especially on fathers who are the sole or main breadwinners.

Then do men enjoy their children less than women do—or are men less fulfilled by being parents? No, not at all. For example, in mid-life fathers are not more likely than mothers to regret having had children or to be dissatisfied with their current relationships with their adult children.[85] In the large national surveys involving more than 12,000 parents, fathers are just as likely as mothers to say they enjoy spending time with their children.[86] Even though mothers spend the most time with the children, they don't say their time with the kids is more meaningful. In fact, in surveys with almost 27,000 adults, men are more likely than women to say that being a parent makes them happy.[83,86] Men are also more likely than employed women to say they want to spend more time with their children—and to feel guilty about not having more time.[32] And as we will see in the next chapter, after a divorce, most men are deeply upset because they are apart from their children.

Box 4.9 Ask a man: Work and family

1. When you were young, what did you hope for in terms of work, money, and family?
2. If money hadn't mattered at all, what kind of job would you do? Why?
3. What have you liked least and liked most about your job?
4. What advice would you give your children about work, family, and happiness?
5. Ideally what would you have needed to create a better balance between work and family?
6. What have other people misunderstood about you in terms of work, money, and family?
7. What impact has your work had on your relationship with your wife and kids?
8. How would you compare the pleasure you get from your job versus from your kids?
9. What are the biggest mistakes you've made related to work and family?
10. What have you lost or had to give up over the years because of your work?

If you want to do another little experiment to see how men feel about being fathers, use the questions in Box 4.9 to interview several dads you know. Afterward, you can tell each dad about the research and see how it matches his experiences.

DENSE AND DUMB: MEN LACK RELATIONSHIP SKILLS, EVEN WITH THEIR KIDS

How do you feel about this joke: "Why don't men show their true feelings? Because they don't have any." And what messages do these book titles convey: *Men Are from Mars, Women Are from Venus,*[87] *You Just Don't Understand: Men and Women in Conversation.*[88] Now, go back and substitute the name of any minority group in place of the word men. Are you laughing—or cringing?

The male-bashing myth underlying these kinds of books and jokes is pretty cringe-worthy: Men are inferior to women when it comes to communicating, empathizing, managing relationships, and being in touch with feelings—theirs or anyone else's. In the school of human communication and relationships, men are in kindergarten. Women are in graduate school. Presumably, this "dense and dumb" app has been installed in boys as well as in men.

These unfounded notions carry forward, of course, into insulting assumptions about men's relationships with their own children. Dads can't communicate, emotionally connect, or empathize with their kids like moms can. Dads don't pick up on their children's feelings and don't know how to respond sensitively. They feel uncomfortable if their children turn to them to share their feelings or to talk about anything personal or emotional. If the kids want to talk about cars, sports, money, grades, movies, politics, or other relatively impersonal topics, then dad will do just fine. But if children have problems with a friend, have questions about dating, or just feel down, then dad is not their go-to guy. When it comes to empathy, communication, and compassion departments, most dads are dunderheads.

Because these beliefs are deeply embedded in our society, let's look closely at two of the most famous books that promoted those ideas—books that were international bestsellers for decades and are still sometimes cited in the media and in college textbooks.

Back in 1982 Carol Gilligan, a Harvard psychology professor, wrote *In A Different Voice,* a book about her own small research studies. Her conclusion was that males and females have very different ways of making moral, ethical decisions.[89] Presumably, women and girls have an "ethics of care" that boys and men lack. Males are mainly concerned about rules and principles without much concern for their impact on people. Males are not as empathetic, as cooperative, or as concerned about other people as females. In her own defense, Gilligan, now 85, says she never meant that females were superior to males.[90] Still, that *is* how her wildly popular study was, and still is, generally interpreted. The impact of her book was huge. Even in 2019, Gilligan was described as a "feminist rock star and academic celebrity" in the prestigious *New York Times.*[90] And as recently as 2021, a blog on a popular website claimed that Gilligan's findings were well-supported by "the research," by which the blogger meant two small studies conducted more than two decades ago.[91]

But there's a catch: Gilligan was wrong. According to more than 50 years of research on these topics, females are not more empathetic, compassionate, cooperative, or concerned about other people's feelings than males.[92–97] It is true that males are more physically aggressive than females. But females are *more* aggressive than males when it comes to another form of aggression—relational aggression, which is more emotionally devastating than a physical fight.[81] In fact, relational aggression is one of the factors that contribute to teenage girls' depression and suicide. This kind of female aggression includes: in-person verbal bullying, insults and attacks, cyber bulling on social media, social ostracism, cruel text messages, hateful gossip, circulating embarrassing pictures, and "ghosting"—refusing to respond to any messages or calls, treating the person as if she did not exist and was not even worthy of a written response. As for the insulting belief that males are less concerned than females about how other people feel, how about this: In 109 research studies, young teenage girls did more cyber bullying than boys. It was only in the late teenage years that boys caught up with girls in cyber bullying.[98]

As for men being inferior to women in communicating, maybe no book has done as much damage as John Grey's best seller, *Men Are from Mars, Women Are from Venus*.[99] First published in 1992 and revised in 2012, accompanied by workbooks and hundreds of workshops for couples, the book's message is clear: Men and women don't communicate well with one another. Why? Because men are in communication kindergarten. No contest. Game over. Grey's book has sold more than 15 million copies, spent nearly two years on bestseller lists in the early 1990s, and is still selling well and highly ranked on amazon.

What does the research say about this "Mars and Venus" research? Simply this: Nonsense. There are no significant gender differences in communication styles between men and women.[93,100,101] Mocking Grey's claims, Janet Hyde, a social scientist who has studied this topic for decades, sums it up like this: "Men are from South Dakota. Women are from North Dakota."[94] Except for the physical aggression, researchers have not found significance differences between men and women on *any* behavior, including empathy and communication styles.[101,102]

On that note, tell the daughters whose comments are in Box 4.10 that their dads lack empathy, compassion, and communication skills. Did their

---

Box 4.10 Fathers and daughters discussing sex and love

"I've always gone to my dad when I need to talk about sex or relationships. A few weeks ago, my dad sent me an e-mail about how I need to change the way I communicate with my boyfriend. He's always been helpful that way."

"My dad is the one who helped me realize I was in a dead-end relationship. He talked to all of us girls about sex, birth control, tampons, having our periods—all of it. As a teenager, at first, I was a little embarrassed; but I'm glad he did. I expect my future husband to do the same for our daughters."

When I broke up with my longtime boyfriend, my dad sat on the couch and let me put my head in his arms while I cried and cried. He also came to me during that week when I was falling apart and told me everything would be fine. Even though I was just a teenager, dad never acted as if it was just "puppy love."

I was surprised when he talked about being hurt by women when he was a young man. I don't think of him as vulnerable or fragile in any way. He's a fairly famous surgeon. Everyone is kind of intimidated by him. I had never heard him say he felt inadequate or admitted his faults.

fathers accidentally stumble into a store where someone forced them to buy communication and empathy apps?

Let's not get off track here. The research is not saying there are no differences at all in how men and women communicate. For example, males are less likely than females to express their feelings by crying in front of another person. Why? Because our society drums it into little boys' heads from the time they are toddlers that "boys don't cry." And are there men who are terrible at communicating or have very little compassion or empathy for others, including their own children? You bet. And the same is true for some women. But that doesn't change the fact that, according to decades of research, males and females are far more alike than different in these regards.

CONCLUSION

As we've seen through this chapter, the negative myths and demeaning stereotypes about fathers begin long before they become parents. The myths of maternal instinct, the hard-wired "mother" brain, and women's hormonal superiority put dads behind in the parenting race from the get-go. Then we heap on more false ideas about men being lazy slouches on couches who selfishly dump the parenting responsibilities on their wives. And if we're all stirred up about women doing most of the childcare and housework, we go hunting for a villain. With negative father stereotypes clouding our vision, we think we already know who the villain is before we even start looking for evidence: fathers.

American men and women make sacrifices when they have children—especially compared to parents in other rich countries where family-friendly policies make parenting a lot easier. Parenthood is sometimes a plate of pits, not a bowl of cherries. And that is just as true for fathers as for mothers. But the way to deal with those pits is not to villainize dads or to see moms as passive victims who are conned, outfoxed, or bamboozled by their husbands or by a sexist society that is working against them. The way forward is to change those beliefs, policies, and individual choices that contribute to the frustrations and troubles that fathers and mothers encounter. As the old saying: "It ain't so much the things that people don't know that makes trouble in this world, as it is the things that people know that just ain't so."

ANSWERS TO THE QUIZZES

Box 4.1   All are false
Box 4.2   All are false except #2
Box 4.4   1, 2, and 4 are false
Box 4.5   All are false except #2

REFERENCES

1. Hrdy S. *Mothers and Others: The Evolutionary Origins of Mutual Understanding.* Belknap Press; 2009.
2. Stone L. *The Rise of Childless America.* Institute of Family Studies, University of Virginia; 2020.
3. Goldin C. *Career & Family: Women's Century Long Journey Toward Equity.* Princeton University; 2021.
4. CDC. *National Survey of Family Growth.* Centers For Disease Control; 2020.
5. Rybinska A, Morgan P. Childless expectations and childlessness over the life course. *Soc Forces.* 2019;97:1571–1602.
6. Piotrowski K. How many parents regret having children. *Plos One.* 2021;July 21, 2121.
7. Newport F, Wilke J. *Desire for Children Still Norm in U.S.* Gallup Organization; 2013.
8. CDC. *Gestational Surrogacy Statistics.* Centers for Disease Control and Prevention; 2017.
9. CDC. *National Vital Statistics Reports.* Vol 64. Centers for Disease Control and Prevention; 2016:5.
10. Gross C, Marcussen K. Postpartum depression in mothers and fathers. *Sex Roles.* 2017;76:290–305.
11. Finkelhor D. *Childhood Victimization.* Oxford University Press; 2014.
12. Abraham E, Feldman R. The neurobiology of human allomaternal care: Implication for fathering and children's social development. *Physiol Behav.* 2018;193:25–34.
13. Machin A. *The Life of Dad: The Making of the Modern Father.* Simon & Schuster; 2018.
14. Weisman O, Feldman R. Oxytocin administration to parent enhances infant physiological and behavioral readiness for social engagement. *Biol Psychiatry.* 2012;July:21–30.
15. Yaniv A, et al. Affiliation, reward and immune biomarkers coalesce to support synchrony during periods of bond formation in humans. *Brain Behav Immun.* 2016;4:4–5.
16. Corpuz R, Rugental D. Life history and differences in male testosterone: Response to first-time fatherhood. *Horm Behav.* 2020;120:21–34.
17. Varela N, et al. Cortisol and blood pressure levels decrease in fathers during the first hour of skin-to-skin contact with their premature babies. *Acta Paediatr.* 2018;107:628–632.
18. Atzil S, Hendler T, Sharon O, Winetraub Y, Feldman R. Synchrony and specificity in the maternal and paternal brain. *Child Adolesc Psychiatry.* 2012;51:798–811.
19. Swaim J, Loberbaum J. Imaging the human parental brain. In: Bridges R, ed. *Neurobiology of the Parental Brain.* Academic Press; 2008:83–92.
20. Abraham E. Father's brain is sensitive to childcare experiences. *Psychol Cogn Sci.* 2014;111:3792–9797.
21. Newland L, Freeman H, Coyle D. *Emerging Topics on Father Attachment.* Routledge; 2011.

22. Van Ijzendoorn M, Vereijken C, Kranenburg M, Walraven M. Assessing attachment security with the Attachment Q Sort: Meta-analytic evidence for the validity of the observer AQS. *Child Dev*. 2004;75:1188–1213.

23. Kochanska G, Kim S. Early attachment organization with both parents: Infancy to middle childhood. *Child Dev*. 2012;83:1–14.

24. Van Ijzendoorn J, Wolff M. In search of the absent father—meta-analyses of infant-father attachment. *Child Dev*. 1997;68:604–609.

25. Fabricius W, Redlich A, Quas J. Attachment and parenting time for children under three years of age. In: Dwyer J, ed. *The Oxford Handbook of Developmental Psychology and the Law*. Oxford University Press; 2022:104–121.

26. NICHD. *The Effects of Infant Child Care on Infant-Mother Attachment Security*. National Institute of Child Health and Human Development; 1997.

27. Zeanah C, Emde R. Attachment disorders in infancy and childhood. In: Rutter M, ed. *Child and Adolescent Psychiatry*. Blackwell; 1994:490–504.

28. Waters E. Are we asking the right questions about attachment? *Fam Court Rev*. 2012;49:474–482.

29. Bretherton I. Fathers in attachment theory. In: Newland L, Freeman H, Coyl D, eds. *Emerging Topics in Father Attachment*. Routledge; 2011:9–24.

30. Lockman D. *All the Rage: Mothers, Fathers and the Myth of Equal Partnership*. Harper; 2019.

31. Bianchi S, Robinson J, Milkie M. *Changing Rhythms of the American Family*. Sage; 2006.

32. Barroso A. *Gender Gaps in Sharing Household Responsibilities Persist Amid Pandemic*. Pew Research Center; 2021.

33. Bianchi S, Sayer L, Milkie M, Robinson J. Housework: Who did or does or will do it and how much does it matter? *Soc Forces*. 2012;91:55–61.

34. BLS. *Employment Characteristics of Families: 2018*. Bureau of Labor Statistics: USDL 190666; 2019.

35. Parker K, Wang W. *Modern Parenthood*. Pew Research Center. March 14, 2013.

36. Parker K, Livingston G. *Seven Facts about American Dads*. Pew Research Center; 2017.

37. Horowitz J. *Who Does More at Home Work When Both Parents Work?* November 5. Pew Research Center; 2015.

38. Cha Y, Weeden K. Overwork and the slow convergence in gender gap in wages. *Am Sociol Rev*. 2014;79:457–484.

39. Weeden K, Cha Y, Bucca M. Long work hours, part-time work and trends in the gender gap in pay. *Russell Sage Found J Soc Sci*. 2016;2:71–102.

40. Coontz S. Why gender equality stalled. *New York Times*. 2013:B 1.

41. Bolotny V, Emanuel N. Why do women earn less than men? *Harvard University, Working Paper, July 5, 2019*. Published online 2021.

42. Kwon K, Akar G. Have gender differences in commuting been shrinking or persistent? *Int J Sustain Transp*. 2021;55:12–20.

43. Brenan M. *Record-High 56% of U.S. Women Prefer Working to Homemaking*. Gallup Poll; 2019.

44. Wang W. Mothers and work: what's ideal? Pew Research Center; 2013 (August 19, 2013).

45. Dernberger BP, Gender flexibility, but not equality: Young adults' division of labor preferences. *Sociol Sci.* 2020; 7:117–132.

46. Chesley N, Flood S. Signs of change? At-home and breadwinner parents' housework and child-care time. *J Marriage Fam.* 2017;79:511–534.

47. Bazelon L. *Ambitious Like a Mother: Why Prioritizing Your Career Is Good for Your Kids.* Little Brown; 2022.

48. Coleman J. *The Lazy Husband: How to Get Men to Do More Parenting and Housework.* St. Martin's; 2007.

49. Dunn J. *How Not to Hate Your Husband after You Have Kids.* Little Brown; 2018.

50. Sydra J. Gendered housework. *Work Employ Soc.* 2022;44:1–19.

51. Gupta S, Sayer L, Pearlman J. Educational and type of day differences in mothers' availability for child care and housework. *J Marriage Fam.* 2021;83:786–802.

52. Stafford F. *Panel Study on Income Dynamics.* University of Michigan; 2008.

53. Freeman M. Time use of millennials and generation X. *Mon Labor Rev.* 2022; 44:1–19.

54. Thebaud S, Kornrich S, Ruppanner L. Good housekeeping, great expectations: Gender and housework norms. *Sociol Methods Res.* 50:1186–1214.

55. Brenan M. *Women Still Handle Main Household Tasks.* Gallup Poll; 2019.

56. Pepin J. Marital status and time use: Childcare, housework, leisure and sleep. *Demography.* 2018;55:107–133.

57. BLS. *Time Spent in Primary Activities by Married Mothers and Fathers by Employment Status: 2007–2010.* Bureau of Labor Statistics; 2015:Table 14.

58. Glass J, Andersson M, Simon R. Parenthood and happiness: Effects of work-family reconciliation policies in 22 OECD countries. *Am J Sociol.* 2016;122: 886–929.

59. Huntington S. *Who Are We? Challenges to America's Identity.* Simon & Schuster; 2015.

60. Altintas E, Sullivan O. Trends in father's contribution to housework and childcare under different welfare policy regimes. *Soc Polit.* 2017;24:81–108.

61. Goldin C. Reassessing the gender wage gap. *Milken Inst Rev.* 2016;2015:1–33.

62. Madowitz M. *Calculating the Hidden Cost of Interrupting a Career for Child Care.* Center for American Progress; 2016.

63. Parker K, Stepler R. *Americans See Men as the Financial Providers.* Pew Research Center; 2017.

64. Graf N, Brown A, Patten E. *The Narrowing, but Persistent, Gender Gap in Pay.* Pew Research Center; 2018.

65. NCES. *Degrees Conferred by Race and Sex: 2019.* National Center for Education Statistics; 2022.

66. Mandel H, Lazarus A. Contextual effects on the gendered division of housework: A cross-country analysis. *Sex Roles.* 2021;85:205–220.

67. Pencavel J. *Diminishing Returns at Work: The Consequences of Long Working Hours.* Oxford University Press; 2018.

68. Kochanek K. Deaths: Final data for 2017. *Natl Vital Stat Rep.* 2019;68:1–16.

69. Nomaguchi K, Johnson W. Parenting stress among low-income and working-class fathers. *J Fam Issues.* 2016;37:1535–1557.

70. Lino M. *Expenditures on Children by Families.* U.S. Department of Agriculture; 2020.

71. Zelizer V. *Pricing the Priceless Child: The Changing Social Value of Children*. Princeton University Press; 1994.

72. NFDA. *Funeral Costs: Trends and Statistics*. National Funeral Directors Association; 2021.

73. Fingerman K, et al. Helicopter parents and landing pad kids: Intense parental support of grown children. *J Marriage Fam*. 2012;74:880–896.

74. Sandberg S, Snyder A, Jang B. Exiting and returning to the parental home for boomerang kids. *J Marriage Fam*. 2015;77:806–818.

75. Fingerman K, Huo M, Birditt K. A decade of research on intergenerational ties. *J Marriage Fam*. 2020;82:383–403.

76. Thorne D, Lawless R, Foohey P. *Bankruptcy Booms for Older Americans*. Consumer Bankruptcy Project; 2018:1–15.

77. Roskam I, et al. Parental burnout around the globe: A 42-country study. *Affect Sci*. 2021;2:58–79.

78. Aumann K, Galinsky E, Mator K. *The New Male Mystique*. Families and Work Institute; 2011.

79. Roskam I, Mikolajczak M. Gender differences in the nature, antecedents and consequences of parental burnout. *Sex Roles*. 2020;83:485–498.

80. Twenge J, Campbell W, Foster C. Parenthood and marital satisfaction: A meta-analytic review. *J Marriage Fam*. 2003;65:574–583.

81. Heimlich R. *Satisfaction with Family Life*. Pew Research Center; 2011.

82. White M, Dolan P. Accounting for the richness of daily activities. *Psychol Sci*. 2009;20:1000–1008.

83. Wolfinger N. *Does Having Children Make People Happier?* December 10, 2018. Institute of Family Studies; 2018.

84. Moore J, Abetz J. What do parents regret about having children? *J Fam Issues*. 2018;40:390–412.

85. DeVries H, Kerrick S, Oetinger M. Satisfactions and regrets of midlife parents. *J Adult Dev*. 2007;14:6–15.

86. Musick K, Meier A, Flood S. How parents fare: mothers' and fathers' subjective well-being in time with children. *Am Sociol Rev*. 2016;81:1069–1095.

87. Gray J. *Men Are from Mars, Women Are from Venus*. Harper Collins; 1992.

88. Tannen D. *You Just Don't Understand: Men and Women in Conversation*. Harper Collins; 1990.

89. Gilligan C, Machung A. *In a Different Voice: Psychological Theory and Women's Development*. Harvard University; 1982.

90. Green P. Carefully smash the patriarchy. *New York Times*. March 18, 2019:1.

91. Vinney C. Carol Gilligan's theory and a woman's sense of self. verywellmind.org, August 30, 2021.

92. Eisenberg N, Lennon R. Sex differences in empathy. *Psychol Bull*. 1983;94:100–131.

93. Barnett N, Rivers C. *Same Difference: How Gender Myths Hurt Our Relationships*. Basic Books; 2004.

94. Hyde J. The gender similarities hypothesis. *Am Psychol*. 2005;60:581–592.

95. Walker L. Gender and morality. In: Killen M, Smetana J, eds. *Handbook of Moral Development*. Erlbaum; 2006:93–115.

96. Koestner R, Franz C, Weinberger J. The family origins of empathic concern: A 26-year longitudinal study. *Personal Soc Psychol.* 1990;58:709–718.

97. Balliet D, Li N, Macfarlan S, Van Vugt M. Sex differences in cooperation: A meta-analytic review of social dilemmas. *Psychol Bull.* 2011;137:881–909.

98. Barlett C, Boyne S. A meta-analysis of sex differences in cyber-bullying behavior. *Aggress Behav.* 2014;40:474–488.

99. Gray J. *Men Are from Mars, Women Are from Venus: The Classic Guide to Understanding the Opposite Sex.* Harper; 2012.

100. Carothers B, Reis H. Men and women are from earth: Examining the latent structure of gender. *J Pers Soc Psychol.* 2012;104:385–407.

101. Maccoby E, Jacklin C. *The Psychology of Sex Differences.* Stanford University Press; 1974.

102. Eliot L. *Pink Brain Blue Brain.* Houghton Mifflin; 2009.

DIVORCED DADS

DAD DUMPED MOM AND WORSE

DOI: 10.4324/9781003324003-5

Although she did not intend to, Former First Lady of the United States, Michelle Obama, insulted millions of divorced dads in a 2019 interview with the television host, Stephen Colbert.[1] What happened? How could a dedicated advocate for families demean fathers? Let's see.

Trying to describe the damage that President Trump had done to the country, Obama compared Trump to an irresponsible divorced father whose teenage children were with him on a weekend visit: "We (Americans) come from a broken family. We're teenagers. We're a little unsettled. Sometimes you spend weekends with divorced dad that feels like it's fun, but then you get sick — that's what America is going through. We're kind of living with divorced dad right now." The audience laughed and Colbert (no slouch himself in advocating for children) went on to impersonate a divorced dad giving his children keys to the car and pointing them in the direction of the liquor cabinet.

Unfortunately, Michele Obama's comments and Colbert's response reinforced many demeaning beliefs about the divorced dad: He's an immature, irresponsible blockhead who recklessly exposes his kids to danger—all for the sake of being seen as their fun-loving friend. But if they get sick or need his care and help, dad is a helpless, clueless fool. Mom is the grownup who makes kids do the "un-fun" things that protect and benefit them. If people as influential and enlightened as Michele Obama and Colbert unintentionally promote negative views about divorced fathers in front of millions of people, then many of us are probably making the same mistake. Can you imagine Obama or Colbert making similar comments or mocking single or divorced mothers?

So what? Does it really matter that famous people, or the rest of us, make insulting remarks or tell demeaning jokes about divorced fathers? Turns out, it does matter and not just to the tender sensibilities of those dads. As we discussed earlier, myths and stereotypes about any group are fueled by these kinds of small, seemingly insignificant events, not just by the larger, more obvious forms of discrimination against them. In anti-racism training, these less noticeable yet powerful acts are called micro-aggressions. And while we shame and scold divorced dads for not doing right by their children, we often fail to recognize the real victims of our false beliefs about divorced fathers: the children we think we're protecting.

Mom and dad are grownups who presumably can see through some of these false beliefs. But children are more gullible and vulnerable to being harmed by negative stereotypes about divorced fathers—stereotypes they hold long before their own parents separate. At risk here are no small number of children. Nearly half of the married parents who once said "I do" say "I don't" before their children turn eighteen. And almost half of the parents never get to the "I do" stage before their breakup.[2]

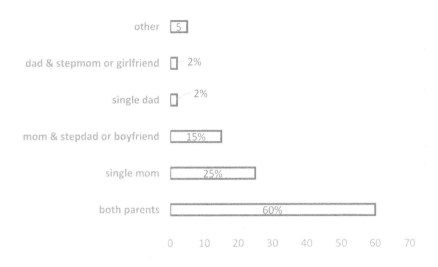

Families with Children

Let's start with the quiz in Box 5.1 to get in touch with our beliefs about divorced fathers.

Box 5.1 Are you fooling yourself: Divorced dads

Which ones do you think are true?

1. Men are the ones who usually leave the marriage.
2. Most divorced men refuse to pay child support.
3. Most dads are far better off financially than their ex-wives.
4. The main reason people divorce is because the husband cheated.
5. Most divorced men enjoy their child-free lives.
6. Most children pretty quickly get over missing their dads.
7. Child support money has more impact on kids than fathering time.
8. Children raised by single dads generally have poor outcomes.
9. Most dads' relationships with their kids are not damaged by ivorce.
10. Men recover from divorce more quickly than their ex-wives.

How many did you think were true? The correct answer is zero. Let's dive into the research that shows why these popular beliefs are hogwash.

WHO WALKS OUT? DAD TRADED MOM IN FOR A NEWER MODEL

> **Box 5.2 Some unexpected Amazon deliveries[3-5]**
>
> The girl was 17 and pregnant. So she and the 19-year-old father got married. Less than 18 months later, they divorced. Two years after that, the biological father gave up his custody rights so the mom's new husband could adopt the young son. Maybe it seemed the right thing to do at the time for the child. He and his son never saw each other again. Decades passed. The son graduated from Princeton, married, had four children, and became rich. Then, six months before their 25th wedding anniversary, the shocking news appeared on the front page of the *National Enquirer:* He was having an affair with a married mother of three. More mindboggling still, his mistress showed his sexy texts and talked about his lewd selfies with her oldest brother. The brother then sold the texts to the *Enquirer.* (What? You mean your sibling wouldn't do that?) The man's wife ended up with a $38 billion in their divorce settlement, making her one of the three richest women and most generous philanthropists on Earth.
>
> Fast forward two years. In 2021 that now wealthy 51-year-old ex-wife married a "younger" man—a 46-year-old high school teacher. At 57, the billionaire and his 51-year-old ex-mistress were still together, though not married. His mother and stepfather were still together after 53 years. But his biological father had died, just two years after learning from a journalist who his son was—Jeff Bezos, founder of Amazon and second richest man in the world.

Highly publicized divorces of wealthy, famous men like Jeff Bezos, Tiger Woods, and Woody Allen make it easier to believe that dads are almost always the villains and moms are the victims, as Boxes 5.2 and 5.3 illustrate. But how true is that? Not very, according to the research.[6-8] Two-thirds of all divorces are initiated by the wife. In fact, some husbands say they are stunned when their wife announces the marriage is over. They didn't see it coming. This might seem hard to believe until we consider the reasons most women say they call it quits—reasons that initially might not have seemed that serious to their husbands. Most wives say they leave their marriages because they feel unfulfilled emotionally, no longer share the same values or goals with their husbands, and cannot resolve their ongoing disagreements about the two topics most couples argue most about—children and money. Many also feel their husband is too immature and has terrible communication skills. The bottom line is that most wives want out because the relationship no longer meets their needs. Although infidelity also sinks marriages, cheating is usually a symptom, not the primary cause of the breakup.

The fact that women are the ones who typically call it quits doesn't mean they are necessarily to blame for the divorce. Maybe women are more willing to pull the plug on a dying or dead relationship. Or maybe men are more willing to put up with a lousy marriage because the divorce laws in their state demote dads to every-other-weekend "uncles." Rummaging through a couple's past to find the cause can be harder than trying to put toothpaste back in the tube. Mark Twain's amusing story makes the point: A child saw a man stump his big toe. In terrible agony, the disoriented fellow stumbled forward, accidentally tripped over a root, and fell headfirst into a dry, deep well where he died on impact. When asked what caused the man's death, the child confidently replied: He stubbed his toe. Harder still is getting spouses who are, in fact, to blame for destroying their marriage to admit "who done it." Take the joke about the wife who fatally shot her husband on their fifteen-story balcony before his body slumped over the railing and fell to the street below. Denying that she was the cause of his death, she calmly explained that "it was the bullet and the fall that killed him—not me."

The point is that we shouldn't let ourselves be duped into believing that husbands are almost always to blame for divorce—or that we can always know why their marriage eventually tumbled to its death in the metaphorical "well."

THE CHEATERS: DADS, OF COURSE

Box 5.3 Google this

Once upon a time, there were once two billionaire fathers who worked at Google and went through divorces in 2015. But that is where their stories diverge.

The first father was Scott Hassan, the unofficial third founder of Google. He sent his wife of 13 years a short text message announcing that he was divorcing her. She claims she was shocked and thought he was kidding. He claims she knew the marriage was over and had stooped to telling their kids he had cheated on her. At one point in their ongoing legal battle, he publicly admitted that "in a moment of frustration" he created a revenge website in her name and posted embarrassing information about her former lovers. Even five years after separating, they were still battling in court over money.[9]

The second father was Sergey Brin, co-founder of Google, and his wife, Anne Wojcicki, founder of the genetic testing company *23andMe*.[10] After eight years of marriage, Brin, then 40, cheated with a 27-year-old employee. Despite the billions of dollars involved in the divorce and worldwide publicity surrounding the affair, Brin and Wojcicki managed to be friendly enough to co-parent their two children. Sergey eventually remarried—no, not to his ex-lover—and Anne, still single, had a third child through sperm donation.

Billionaire, high-profile divorce stories like the ones in Box 4.3 can lead us to believe that husbands are almost always the cheaters. Even our jokes play into this belief: The dad's divorce lawyer tells him that, as they prepare things to go to court, he needs to get his affairs in order. And the dad asks: "Alphabetically or by age?"

Box 5.4 Fooling yourself: Who cheats?

Which of these statements do you believe are true?

1. Husbands cheat far more often than wives.
2. Men almost always cheat with women much younger than their wives.
3. College-educated couples cheat less often than other couples.
4. Very religious and politically conservative couples are the most faithful.
5. Couples in their 20s and 30s cheat much more than older married couples.

Considering your answers to the quiz in Box 5.4, when you picture a cheating spouse, what pops into your head? A man? Someone on the liberal end of the religious spectrum? A person in their twenties or thirties? An adult without a college degree? If that's what you imagine, you're on the wrong track and you probably didn't score well on the quiz because all the statements are false.[11–13]

Let's start with a more accurate picture of the typical cheater.[11–13] The cheater is almost as likely to be the wife as the husband if for couples between the ages of 18 and 50. Somewhere between 10% and 15% of spouses in that age bracket cheat. And husbands are not significantly more likely than wives to have a much younger lover. As for religion, the most conservative and evangelical couples are not more faithful than more liberal, secular Americans. And if you were hoping a college degree was an infidelity insurance policy, you can throw the diploma out the window. Well-educated spouses are not significantly more faithful than less-educated couples.

As for the security and fidelity in older marriages, when couples pass fifty, things start changing—for the worse, not the better.[14,15] With age, cheating gets worse, especially for men. By the time they reach their 60s, nearly 25% of husbands and 15% of wives have cheated. With Viagra for men, hormone supplements to boost libido for women, and longer lifespans, the sexual landscape for older couples has changed. And as infidelity has increased for those over 50, so has divorce. The rate for those over 65 has tripled since 1990 to 6%. Surprisingly, nearly a third of the people who divorce after

50 have been married at least 30 years. On the other hand, wealthier and college-educated couples over 50 are about half as likely to divorce as their less educated counterparts. And, if it's any comfort in terms of not being caught off guard, more than half of the "gray" divorced couples have been divorced two or three times already.

As for negative stereotypes about divorced fathers and religious couples, the saga of Jerry Falwell, Jr. and his wife, Becki turns many of those stereotypes on their heads. Falwell is one of the world's most famous and influential evangelical leaders and was president of the most famous conservative fundamentalist colleges in the world, Liberty University in Lynchburg, Virginia. Becki Falwell also came from an evangelical family. Together, they were "the" Christian fundamentalist power couple until their downfall in 2020—a downfall that garnered international attention. And as we can see from Box 5.5, their situation echoes what the research on infidelity has been telling us all along about our mistaken beliefs about men, religious conservatives, and college-educated spouses.[16,17]

The good news here is that if you're imagining that most married people are cheating, you're wrong. Even though cell phones, dating apps, and social media should make it easier than ever to cheat, married people today cheat *less* than people did back in the 1950s and 60s. How many of the married people you know might cheat at some time during their marriage? Two in ten.

Box 5.5 The pool boy and the famous evangelical's wife

Becki Tilley at 18 dropped out of the most famous fundamentalist Christian college in the world, Liberty University, and two years later married Jerry Falwell Jr., son of the university's founder. Eventually becoming America's most influential, fundamentalist couple, Falwell Jr. succeeded his dad as university president. They hobnobbed with the rich and famous, including the American President at that time, Donald Trump. Then the bubble burst. At 45, Becki confessed to Jerry: She had been cheating with a former pool boy, a man 20 years her junior, the age of their eldest son. Over the next several years, Jerry made her lover the manager of his hotel, paid for his expensive vacations, let him use their private jet, and invited him to their son's wedding. Despite their efforts to keep it from going public, the lover eventually spilled the beans and wrote a book about the seven-year affair, Falwell Jr. was fired as Liberty's president, as was his eldest son who was vice president of operations. In their first public interview in 2021, Becki happily proclaimed: "We're together more than any couple you will ever meet in your life. He forgave me, and that's what Jesus teaches, forgiveness."

But even if husbands are not more unfaithful than their wives, isn't it still true that most men leave their wives for a younger woman? No, not according to our census data.[18] In first marriages, only 5% of men *and women* marry someone at least ten years younger. If we want to criticize or joke about husbands "robbing the cradle," then women and men are equal "robbers." On the other hand, in second marriages, men are more likely (20%) to marry a woman at least 10 years younger. Still, that means that, even the second time around, 80% of men do *not* marry a very young woman.

Men generally get remarried a year or two before their ex-wives.[19] This helps explain why children usually have a stepmother in their lives before they have a stepfather. This is not especially surprising since divorced dads are generally much lonelier and have more free time for dating than their ex-wives if they have been demoted to every-other-weekend parents. Nevertheless, men are not more likely than their ex-wives to eventually remarry. Two-thirds of divorced men and women say "I do—again," with white, college-educated adults more likely than other Americans to remarry.[20]

Do some dads dump their wives for younger women? Do some fathers marry a woman close to the age of their adult children? Do some wives carry on an affair for years, even when their husband knows, or strongly suspects, or might even participate in what is going on? You bet. But we don't want to let ourselves be hoodwinked into believing that these media grabbing, riveting stories, hyped by TV docudramas and best-selling books, reflect how the vast majority of married husbands and wives behave.

MONEY: DAD WINS, MOM LOSES

When we think about the lifestyles of divorced dads and their ex-wives, what pops into our heads? Maybe something like this: Dad has a nice place to live, a late-model car with a spotless interior, and food in the fridge from the most expensive stores. He shops at upscale stores and goes on cool vacations. Mom lives in a fixer-upper house, drives an old car with kids' food stains on the seats, and shops with coupons at discount stores.

How far off the mark is this picture? As we might guess, most divorced husbands and wives feel they got ripped off when it came to money. And in terms of animosity and resentment, the actual financial facts don't matter here as much as people's feelings. Some adult children tell us that even decades after their parents' divorce, they still feel bitter and complain about getting ripped off financially.[21] These dads might feel like Ken in the Barbie doll joke: A shopper in a toy store asks the salesperson why the "Divorced Barbie" package costs $100 when all the other Barbie packages only cost $19.95? The clerk replies, "Because Divorced Barbie comes with Ken's car, Ken's house, Ken's boat, Ken's dog, Ken's cat, and Ken's furniture." On the other hand, mothers often have reason to feel that their "Ken" never fully compensated them for the years of lost income or damage to their careers from taking years away from work to stay home with the children. These ex-wives may feel like taking out a big ad: "Wedding dress for sale. Worn once—by mistake."

Who really ends up financially better off—the man or his ex? Before we look at the research, we need to understand why answering that question is complicated.[22,23] First, researchers compare divorced women as a group to divorced men as a group. They are *not* comparing men and women who were formerly married *to each other*. Second, most researchers don't consider couples' educational levels. This matters because college-educated couples usually have more similar standards of living after they separate than less educated couples. Third, most researchers only compare the parents' incomes which isn't the best way to get a picture of their actual standard of living. For example, the mother's standard of living might be higher than it initially appears from her income and child support payments if she continues living in the family's home and pays lower taxes due to child-relaxed tax benefits. Fourth, even when children live with their father 25%–30% of the year, he has to send the same amount of child support money to their mother even though it is costing him more to have the children live with him that frequently. In the only study that has ever considered all of these factors, fathers ended up with $25 a month more than mothers ($45 in 2023 dollars).[22]

Then too, researchers usually compare men's and women's incomes in the first year or two after divorce—the time when the income gap is greatest because most women are re-establishing themselves in the workforce.

Moreover, most divorced men and women remarry which generally boosts the woman's standard of living but lowers the man's.[24] For example, five years after divorce, women are about 3% better off and men about 6% better off financially than when they were married.[25] Then too, much of the older research doesn't reflect the fact that the younger generation of women is in better financial shape than older women, which leaves them in a better position after divorce. For example, women under the age of 35 now earn 90% of what men earn when they work the same jobs and similar hours.[26] And women are now more likely than men to earn an undergraduate degree.[27] This puts many women in a better position financially after divorce than older research studies show.

Keeping these limitations in mind, what does the research tell us?[20] To begin with, a man or a woman needs to have 30% more money after divorce to maintain their former standard of living. As the saying goes, "Two can live more cheaply than one." Divorce is almost always a big step down financially for men and women. Still, women usually live on 30% less money and men on 20% less money than they lived on during their marriage. Yet there is one group of mothers who take a much greater hit financially than their ex-husbands—and who do not recover as the years pass. These are the very poorest couples with the least education—the couples who also have the highest divorce rates.[23] As long as they stay married, they can generally squeak by without falling in poverty. But once they separate, almost one in five of these mothers and children fall into poverty—and, unlike their ex-husbands, most of these mothers never manage to lift themselves or their children out of poverty.

Who or what is to blame when mothers are worse off than their ex-husbands? Researchers are pretty clear on this point.[13,23] The major culprits are the job decisions the man and woman make before they ever meet one another and after having children together. Compared to women whose marriages last, divorced women are less educated, earn less money before and during the marriage, and quit work more often after they have kids. Predictably then, these mothers have a harder time catching up to their ex-husbands' incomes after their divorce.

Are some men shifty, selfish scoundrels who somehow manage to shortchange their ex-wives and their children financially? Sure. But these situations are rare. Keep in mind that almost all state laws require the husband to give 50% of all the assets acquired during the marriage to his wife—including half of the money in his retirement accounts. So, before we jump to the conclusion that the man is generally to blame when his ex-wife's standard of living is lower than his, we need to consider the job-related and childcare decisions they made during their marriage—choices that, in the wake of their divorce, each of them might wish they could erase by hitting the alt/delete buttons.

DEADBEAT DADS: MOST DADS ARE

> **Box 5.6 A penny for your thoughts[28]**
>
> The daughter just graduated from high school. She and her dad had not had much of a relationship since her parents' divorce when she was young. Still, he faithfully mailed his child support checks. But this time, he delivered the money in person. He pulled up to his ex-wife's house in a rented trailer and dumped 80,000 pennies in her front yard. When the startled mother rushed out to find out what was going on, the dad yelled, as he drove away, that he was making his final child support payment. When accounts of this mean-spirited episode went viral, he told reporters he was acting out of 18 years of pent-up frustration and that he hadn't meant to drive a further wedge between him and his daughter. Alas, as his daughter told reporters: "It's not just my mom he's trying to embarrass. It's also me and my sister." The daughter and her mom donated $800 to a domestic abuse center.

Let's start with a joke about deadbeat dads: It had been a contentious case, but the judge finally reached a decision and announced to the dad. "I decided to give your wife $800 a week." Relieved, the smiling husband replied: "That's very fair, your honor. Every now and then, I'll try to send her a few bucks myself." This joke and the story in Box 5.6 about the dad who dumped 80,000 pennies in his ex-wife's yard remind us that not all fathers are kind or fair-minded when it comes to paying child support.

But despite the stories that make the headlines or go viral, are most divorced dads deadbeats who refuse to pay child support? No, not according to our census data.[29,30] There are about 3.5 million mothers and fathers who filed official papers that entitle them to child support money. Some were formerly married and then divorced. Others were never married and then separated. Keep in mind that poor and never-married parents often do not fill out the paperwork for child support orders because they know the other parent doesn't have the money to pay. Other parents, formerly married or never married, don't apply for the money because they do not want the other parent involved in their lives or in their children's lives.

For those parents who do have child support orders, if we count divorced and never married men together, about half of them pay every cent, 25% pay most and 25% pay nothing. Most men who pay nothing were never married to their children's mother. These dads are generally living in poverty and suffering from high rates of incarceration, substance abuse, and mental health problems. What's important here is that, if these men could earn enough money to pay what is due, the amount paid would be so small that only 20% of their children would be lifted out of poverty.[31] So, yes, there are "dead-beat" dads. And there are deadbeat moms who do not pay their children's father what is due. In fact, women are no more likely to pay up than men.

But if we're only talking about *divorced* dads, the deadbeat myth runs out of gas.[25] Only 20% of divorced dads pay none of what is due. On average, parents are supposed to pay about $5,800 a year. The average pay is $5,200. Of course, richer parents pay far more than this because child support payments are based on each parent's income. To put this in perspective, child support money only accounts for about 15% of the mother's total income. So why are some divorced dads not paying in full or paying nothing at all? Because, according to the census data, most of them don't have the money. For example, some have lost their jobs or are earning less than what they were earning at the time of the divorce. Still, 80% of them are paying some or all of what is due.[23,24]

So, some divorced fathers have the money but refuse to pay? Yes. Shame on them. But if we keep reinforcing the falsehood that most divorced dads are deadbeats, then shame on us.

MONEY TRUMPS FATHERING: JUST SEND THE CHILD SUPPORT CHECK, DUDE

After their parents' breakup, what benefits kids most—child support money or the quality of their relationship with him? Clearly having both is best. But which matters *most?* This is a very real-life question. Parents, custody evaluators, mediators, lawyers, judges, and legislators who make our custody laws have to decide how high a priority to put on maximizing children's time with their fathers versus maximizing his child support payments. Custody laws also have to specify what the punishments will be for fathers who don't pay up and for mothers who prevent children from spending time with their dad because he isn't paying.

To bring this question into sharper focus, assume you are a judge. The parents have had a temporary, informal custody arrangement for the past twelve months—which is not an uncommon situation in the real world. Now you have to decide how much time these children will be allowed to spend with their father until they reach the age of 18—including the option of having them live half-time with each parent. How much parenting time would you award each father in this hypothetical example?

Larry is a great dad. Put a red cape on him and he'd be Super Dad. His son and daughter adore him. He never shows up late to pick them up, misses any of his weekends with them, or fails to show up at school and sports events. He is very focused on what is going on in their lives. Even though his ex-wife still says he was a lousy husband, she admits he is an A+ parent. The downside is that when it comes to child support money, Larry is a Super Dud, not a Super Dad. Over the past year, his child support payments have been hit or miss. He always sheepishly apologizes, offers lame excuses, and promises to do better. But nothing changes.

Then there is Louis. He gets A+ on the child support report card. He always pays on time. He voluntarily pays for high-ticket items like summer camp and computers—money he is not legally required to spend. Unfortunately, he barely scrapes by with Cs on his parenting report card—along with an occasional F. He often makes excuses for why he can't spend his allotted time with the kids. He fails to show up for some of their most important events. He is not unkind, or mean, or unloving. He's just more tuned out than tuned in. And whenever he disappoints the kids, he tries to make it up by buying expensive gifts. The children say they love him. But he is more like their favorite uncle than a father.

If you are having a hard time deciding, you might still be struggling with the money myths we discussed in an earlier chapter. The take-home message from that research was that children with richer parents are not better off than those from less wealthy families when it comes to emotional, psychological, behavioral problems or drug and alcohol use. Richer parents' kids do tend to make better grades and are more likely to go to college. But that's about the extent of their advantages. With the exception of children who grow up in poverty, family income has far less impact than many of us believe.[32] The bottom line is that the "deposits" a father makes into his children's "heart" accounts are more beneficial than his deposits into their savings accounts. You can bank on it.

KIDS DON'T MISS THEIR DADS—NOT MUCH AND NOT FOR LONG

One of the more heartbreaking beliefs is that most children don't miss living with their dads after their parents split up—or if they do miss him, they'll get over it pretty quickly. This harkens back to the belief that, even in married families, as long as kids have a good relationship with their mom, dad is pretty insignificant. "Out of sight and out of mind." Right? Wrong, according to what children of divorce tell us. For decades children have consistently told researchers that the worst part of their parents' divorce is being separated from their dad—missing him and longing for the kind of relationship they used to have.[21] As Box 5.7 reminds us, most of these children, even as adults, feel a lot like *E.T.* and Elliot in Steven Spielberg's famous film.[33] They mourn and feel abandoned, longing for the family they once had.

Box 5.7 E.T. Phone home

In *E.T.*, three children and their divorced mother befriend a charming extra-terrestrial who was accidentally left behind by his mothership. Dad and his girlfriend are on vacation in Mexico and the younger son, Elliot, is struggling with his dad's abandoning him. E.T. and Elliot have both been "left behind." Both long for the home they once had. When the spaceship finally returns, E.T. knows Elliot will feel unloved and abandoned *again*. Tenderly he touches Elliott on the forehead and lovingly whispers: "I'll be right here."

Steven Spielberg admits that, even though he was 19 at the time, his parents' divorce had a profound impact on his life and on his movies.[33] His dad allowed Spielberg and his siblings to believe he caused the divorce. And the kids all dumped him. In fact, the mother is the one who cheated and left her husband for their best friend. It took Spielberg, then a divorced father himself, 15 years to reconcile with his father.

As Spielberg admits, fathers come off looking pretty bad in many of his movies. In *Encounters of the Third Kind,* the father destroys the house and ditches his wife and kids to fly away on the aliens' spaceship. And in *War of the Worlds*, the divorced dad has pretty much abandoned his children until aliens try to take over the world. As for *E.T.*, Spielberg says: "It was never meant to be a movie about an extra-terrestrial. It was supposed to be a movie about my mom and dad getting a divorce."[33,34]

DADS DON'T MISS KIDS—AT LEAST NOT FOR LONG

If we buy into the belief that most children aren't profoundly upset by living apart from their dad, then it's easier to believe that their dad feels the same way. And if we are under the spell of the stereotype that most men cheat, leave their wife for a young woman, and have a much higher standard of living than their ex, then divorce must be a "get out of parenting jail free" pass for dads.

If all this is true, then why are men far more likely than their ex-wives to be depressed, suicidal, lonely, and physically and emotionally stressed?[35,36] And if they are having so much fun, why are dads more likely to drink and use drugs and to develop stress-related health problems after the breakup? Indeed, divorced women are no more likely than married women to commit suicide. But divorced men are more than twice as likely as married men to kill themselves.[37] In part, this happens because when men are depressed, they are less likely than depressed women are to seek help.[38,39] And in part, it's because friends and co-workers don't give men as much support as they give women when they're going through or recovering from their divorce.[40] While most children probably have no idea what their father is going through, when they finally become adults, some of them get the picture, as the story in Box 5.8 illustrates.

Why are so many divorced fathers in such bad shape? Mainly because they desperately miss living with their children.[22,35] They also miss their home, the familiar neighborhood, and the friends they once shared with their wives. Many dads also suffer another loss: The family pet. This might seem silly or trivial if you have never been deeply attached to a pet. But these

Box 5.8 What my dad went through: A young adult reflects

After all this time, I finally let my dad tell me his side of the divorce. It made me uncomfortable because I've tried so hard to maintain a positive image of my mother. After much thought, I've decided it's still possible for me to admire her even though I now clearly see now how much suffering she caused my dad. One of his comments cut straight to my heard. He said he wonders if he will ever marry again. The look on his face and tone of his voice showed me how much the divorce had hurt him. I stopped feeling mad at him because I saw him as a man with a lonely heart. I asked him what had made him saddest after the divorce. I thought he would say it was when I ruined his 40th birthday by refusing to be there. Instead, he said the saddest thing was not being allowed to be part of my day-to-day life.

bonds can be extremely powerful and comforting, especially when we're going through something as stressful as divorce. In fact, since almost 70% of Americans own pets, it's more common nowadays for couples to have custody battles over their pets—which is why four states actually have legal guidelines for pet custody disputes.[41]

Of course, after divorce, mothers can also feel sad, depressed, anxious, stressed, or even suicidal. But the fact remains that mothers generally suffer less than fathers in terms of their physical and mental health. Despite these realities, we can see from Box 5.9, many movies continue to feed some of the worst stereotypes about divorced dads.

Box 5.9 The movies: Demeaning divorced dads

Waiting to Exhale Four African American women have been done wrong by their ex-husbands. They are out for revenge, having a rollicking good time plotting their attacks which include setting fire to one ex-husband's car.

First Wives Club Three white women work together plotting ways to destroy their ex-husbands' lives. All their ex's cheated on them with beautiful, young women. The mothers even include their adult children in some of the vengeful attacks against their father and his girlfriend.

The Squid and the Whale A divorced couple and their two sons are struggling through the initial phases of divorce. The dad is a vain professor and once-famous novelist who resents his ex-wife's success as a writer. The mom is dating a sweet man. Dad is hitting on his female graduate student. The teenage son, who initially adores his dad and resents his mom, eventually see his dad for who he is—a selfish, narcissistic, immature jerk.

The lifelong damage to many children's relationships with their dads is unsettling and heartbreaking. Adult children give more emotional support, more money, and more direct care to their divorced mothers than to their divorced fathers.[48,49] And more adult children are estranged from their fathers than from their mothers, many of whom come from divorced families.[50,51] A number of these children rejected their fathers, even though they had a good relationship with him before their parents' divorce. In these situations, the mother said and did things that turned the children against their dad, a situation known as parental alienation.[52–54] Sadly too, when the dad remarries, his children, even as adults, are much more likely to distance themselves or reject him (and his wife) than when their mom remarries. This can even happen when the parents are in their 60s or 70s when they remarry[55] The welcome mat might be out for the stepdad, but not for the stepmom. And watch out for the daughters because they tend to give their dads and stepmoms a much harder time than sons do.[56]

Why not do a little experiment yourself? Take time to interview of few divorced fathers. Choose some who are recently divorced and some who were divorced many years ago. Use the questions in Box 5.10 to get you started. How well do each dad's experiences sync with the research?

Box 5.10 Ask a man: Divorce and remarriage

Take an hour or so to talk with a divorced and remarried father about his divorce or remarriage. How do his feelings and experiences fit with the negative stereotypes of divorced and remarried dads?

1. What was most painful, most hurtful, and most upsetting about what you went through?
2. What do you wish you had known before your divorce & before getting remarried?
3. How did the divorce and then your remarriage affect your relationship with your children?
4. What do you wish you had done differently after the divorce and when you remarried?
5. How do you feel things might have been different if you had been the mother, instead of the father going through these experiences?

SINGLE DADS: MELTING DOWN OR MANNING UP?

After their parents' breakup, almost two and a half million children ended up living with their single dad—four times as many as in 1960. And 12,000 of these children are less than a year old.[42] If we fall for the myth that men are inferior to women as parents, then we would assume that children who get "stuck" living with dad are going to turn out worse than those who live with their single mom. Let's check out that assumption.

Before addressing that issue, we have to understand the differences between single-mother and single-father families.[43] Nearly 70% of single fathers were formerly married to their children's mothers. The reverse is true for single moms, where 70% have never been married. Single dads are also more educated, make more money, and usually have children with only one woman, unlike single moms.

Are these single dads doing a good job parenting on their own? Yes, they are. In fact, their children tend to be doing better than single mothers' children in terms of grades, depression, anxiety, and behavioral problems.[43,44] They are also in better physical health than children living with single mothers or with mothers and stepfathers.[45] Hurrah for the dads.

People who don't want to give single dads credit for good parenting might claim these children are doing better only because their dads have more money than single moms. But that's not the case. First, as we discussed in the last chapter, unless children are living in poverty, their parents' incomes generally don't have much impact on behavioral problems, mental health issues, or social relationships. Second, even after considering the parents' incomes, single fathers' children still had better outcomes than single mothers' children.[46,47]

Let's give credit where it's due. Most single dads raising children on their own are manning up, not melting down. Fortunately, given how many movies portray single moms as admirable and heroic, some movies are slowly getting this message across about single dads.

Box 5.11 The movies: Some loving, lovable divorced dads

Kramer vs. Kramer Without warning, the wife leaves her husband and five year old son to "find herself." The workaholic dad eventually gets so involved in parenting that he gets fired from his demanding job. After a year or so, the mom returns. She goes to court for full custody. The little boy wants to stay with his dad. But the mom wins custody. Then in the final scene, she morphs into a loving mother and allows their son to keep living with his dad.

Mrs. Doubtfire. A mother with a high-stress career divorces her immature, irresponsible, unemployed husband. He's only allowed to see the kids for supervised weekend visits. Heartbroken, he disguises himself as a frumpy, middle-aged woman in order to get his ex-wife to hire him as the nanny. When she discovers the truth, she bans him from seeing the kids at all. After finally landing a job as Mrs. Doubtfire on a children's TV show, the mother allows him to see the kids every day after school until she gets home from work.

The Pursuit of Happyness A well-educated African American father finds himself out of work and is evicted from his apartment after his wife has left him and abandoned their five-year-old son. The dad is desperately trying to find a job, raising his son alone, and studying for his stockbroker license exam. At one point, they end up homeless. In the end, the dad lands a great job and triumphs as a single father. The movie is based on the true story of Chris Gardner, a divorced father in San Francisco, who eventually formed his own multimillion-dollar brokerage firm.

ANSWERS TO THE QUIZZES

Box 5.1 All are false
Box 5.4 All are false

CONCLUSION

Destroying baseless beliefs and stereotypes about divorced dads is a slow, frustrating process. Meanwhile, the people paying the biggest price are the millions of children whose parents have separated. Let's keep two things in mind from the earlier chapters: First, children benefit in countless ways throughout their lives when they have supportive, involved, loving relationships with their dads while they are growing up. And that kind of relationship is very difficult to create or maintain after parents separate. Second, many children from father-absent homes end up having lifelong problems that take a financial and emotional toll on society in terms of higher rates of delinquency and incarceration, drug and alcohol abuse, teenage pregnancy, mental health problems, and reliance on welfare programs. The fact that these fathers are fighting an uphill battle to maintain or strengthen their relationships with their kids *is* a *concern for all of us,* even if we never find ourselves in this situation. So in the next chapter, we will explore the question: After parents separate, how can we help fathers and their children maintain and strengthen their relationships?

REFERENCES

1. Shannon J. Michelle Obama sparks backlash by implying Donald Trump is like a divorced dad. *USA Today, April 17, 2019.* 2019.
2. Census Bureau. *Current Population Survey.* Department of Labor; 2020.
3. Mattioli D. Philanthropist MacKenzie Scott, ex-wife of Jeff Bezos, marries Seattle school teacher. *Wall Street Journal.* March 7, 2021.
4. Rothfeld M. Jeff Bezos is sued by his girlfriend's brother. *New York Times.* February 2, 2020.
5. Stone B. *Amazon Unbound: Jeff Bezos and the Invention of a Global Empire.* Simon & Schuster; 2021.
6. Stewart A, Brentano C. *Divorce: Causes and Consequences.* Yale University; 2006.
7. Rosenfeld M. Who wants the breakup? Gender and breakup in heterosexual couples. In: Alwin D, Felmlee D, Kreager D, eds. *Social Networks and the Life Course.* Springer; 2018:221–243.
8. Hawkins A, Willoughby S, Doherty W. Reasons for divorce and openness to marital reconciliation. *J Divorce Remarriage.* 2012;53:453–463.
9. Kaplan M. Google founder admits he created revenge site against estranged wife. *New York Post.* August 20, 2021.
10. Dowd M. The doyenne of DNA says: Just chillax with your ex. *New York Times.* November 18, 2017.
11. General Social Survey Staff. *Demographics of Infidelity in America.* University of Chicago; 2017.
12. Fincham F, May R. Infidelity in romantic relationships. *Curr Opin Psychol.* 2017;13:70–74.

13. Demo D, Fine M. *Beyond the Average Divorce.* Sage; 2010.
14. Stepler R. *Divorce Rates Climb for America's 50+ Population.* March 9, 2017. Pew Research Center; 2017.
15. Lin I, Brown S, Mellencamp K. The roles of gray divorce and subsequent repartnering for parent-adult relationships. *Gerontology.* 2022;77:212–223.
16. Granda G, Ebner M. *Off the Deep End: Jerry and Becki Falwell and the Collapse of an Evangelical Dynasty.* William Morrow; 2022.
17. Sherman G. Inside Jerry Falwell Jr.'s unlikely rise and precipitous fall at liberty university. *Vanity Fair.* January 24, 2022.
18. Livingston G. *Trying the Knot Again?* December 4, 2014. Pew Research Center; 2014.
19. Livingston G. *The Demographics of Remarriage.* Pew Research Center; 2014.
20. Geiger A, Livingston G. *8 Facts about Love and Marriage in America.* February 13, 2019. Pew Research Center; 2019.
21. Harvey J, Fine M. *Children of Divorce: Stories of Loss and Growth.* Routledge; 2010.
22. Braver S, O'Connell D. *Divorced Dads: Shattering the Myths.* Tarcher/Putnam; 1998.
23. Sayer L. Economic aspects of divorce. In: Fine M and Harvey J, eds. *Handbook of Divorce and Relationship Dissolution.* Erlbaum; 2006:385–406.
24. Duncan G, Hoffman S. Reconsideration of economic consequences of divorce. *Demographics.* 1985;22:485–497.
25. Bayaz G. The effects of union dissolution on the economic resources of men and women: A comparative analysis of Germany and the U.S. 1985–2013. *Ann Am Acad Pol Soc Sci.* 2014;680:235–258.
26. Graf N, Brown A, Patten E. *The Narrowing, but Persistent, Gender Gap in Pay.* Pew Research Center; 2018.
27. NCES. *Degrees Conferred by Race and Sex: 2019.* National Center for Education Statistics; 2022.
28. O'Neill J. Dads dumps 80,000 pennies on estranged daughter's lawn for final child support. *New York Post.* June 12, 2021.
29. Grall T. *Custodial Mothers and Fathers and Their Child Support: 2017.* Vol P60-269. Census Bureau; 2020:1–19.
30. Solomon C. *Child Support: An Overview of Census Data.* Congressional Research Service; 2016.
31. Stirling KSK. Child support: Who bears the burden? *Fam Relat.* 2008;57:376–389.
32. Brooks-Gunn J, Duncan G. *Consequences of Growing up Poor.* Russel Sage Foundation; 1997.
33. Breznican A. Steven Spielberg has lost his father. *Vanity Fair.* August 28, 2020.
34. Cameron J. Spielberg reveals that E.T. started as a story about his parents' divorce. *People.* April 27, 2018.
35. Kaslow F. *Divorced Fathers and Their Families.* Springer; 2013.
36. Braver S, Shapiro J, Goodman M. Consequence of divorce for parents. In: Fine M, Harvey J, eds. *Handbook of Divorce.* Routledge; 2006:313–337.
37. Kposowa A. Marital status and suicide in the National Longitudinal Mortality Study. *J Epidemiol Community Health.* 2000;54:254–261.
38. Oren C, Oren D. Counseling fathers. In: Carlson M, Evans M, Duffey T, eds. *A Counselor's Guide to Working with Men.* Wiley; 2015:233–252.
39. NIMH. *Men and Mental Health.* National Institute of Mental Health; 2021.

40. Stone G. Father postdivorce well-being. *J Divorce Remarriage*. 2007;41:139–150.
41. Willets M An exploratory investigation of companion animal custody disputes following divorce. *J Divorce Remarriage*. 62:1–18.
42. Duffin E. Children living with single divorced parents in 2021. September 30, 2022. Statista.org.
43. Coles R. Single father families: A review of the literature. *J Fam Theory Rev*. 2015;7:144–166.
44. Lee S, Kushner J, Cho S. Effects of parents' gender on children's achievements in single parent families. *Sex Roles*. 2007;56:149–157.
45. Ziol-Guest K, Dunifon R. Complex living arrangements and child health. *Fam Relat*. 2014;63:424–437.
46. Dufur J. Sex differences in parenting in single mother and single father households. *J Marriage Fam*. 2010;72:1092–1106.
47. Clarke-Stewart A, Hayward C. Advantages of father custody and contact for the psychological wellbeing of school-age children. *J Appl Dev Psychol*. 1996;17: 239–270.
48. Fingerman K, Huo M, Birditt K. A decade of research on intergenerational ties. *J Marriage Fam*. 2020;82:383–403.
49. Lin F. Adult children's support of frail parents. *Marriage Fam*. 2008;70:113–128.
50. Coleman J. *Rules of Estrangement: Why Adult Children Cut Ties and How to Heal the Conflict*. Harmony; 2021.
51. Pillemer K. *Fault Lines: Fractured Family Relationships and How to Heal Them*. Avery; 2020.
52. Warshak R. *Divorce Poison: How to Protect Your Family from Bad-Mouthing and Brainwashing*. Harper; 2010.
53. Lorandos D and Bernet W. *Parental Alienation and the Law*. Charles Thomas; 2020.
54. Clawar S. *Parent-Child Reunification: A Guide to Legal and Forensic Strategies*. American Bar Association; 2020.
55. Papernow P. Recoupling in mid-life and beyond: From love at last to not so fast. *Fam Process*. 2018;57:52–69.
56. Nielsen L. Father-daughter relationships: Research and issues. In: Perry A, Mazza C, eds. *Fatherhood in America*. Charles Thomas; 2016:115–152.

SUBVERTING THE STEREOTYPES
AND MASHING THE MYTHS

DOI: 10.4324/9781003324003-6

Throughout this book, we have unpacked and dismantled hundreds of damaging, demeaning myths, and stereotypes about fathers. As we have seen, some of these baseless beliefs and assumptions border on cruel, while others are just downright silly. So now what? What can we do to counter and dismantle these false ideas and assumptions?

Most importantly, why does any of this matter? Are we just trying to be fair or politically correct? Not that those are unworthy goals. But our goal should be to improve the lives of children. Fortunately, decades of research have given us one surefire, no-nonsense way to do that: Strengthen fathers' relationships with their children. First by acknowledging and then by destroying myths and stereotypes that work against those relationships, we are doing what is right for children.

WORKPLACE AND CHILDCARE POLICIES

When Americans finally decided that helping women get ahead in the workforce was important enough, we enacted laws and policies to promote that goal. We also took other steps, including holding the advertising and movie industries, toy manufacturers, and children's book publishers accountable for promoting sexist stereotypes about women and girls. If we sincerely value men as parents and truly want parents to have more freedom in how they divvy up the childcare and income earning in the best interests of their children, then why haven't we taken similar actions relating to dads?

Where should we start? This is a no-brainer, given what other countries have already done. The other 22 richest countries are far ahead in creating policies and laws that support and prioritize fathering. The U.S. comes in dead last.[1] We are the only rich country without guaranteed paternity leave and free or subsidized childcare. Is it any wonder American parents are unhappier, more burned out, and more likely to have second thoughts about having had kids than parents in the other rich countries?[1]

Sweden is the best example of what happens when a country decides to make fathers' relationships with their children a top priority.[2-4] In Sweden the mother and the father are each entitled to 240 days of *paid* leave to care for their child up until the age of eight. Each receives full pay for 200 of those days and 80% of their pay for the other 40 days. These days can be used immediately after the child is born or adopted. Or they can be used to take days off to tend to the children's needs up until the age of eight. If either parent decides not to use their 240 days, they *cannot* transfer their remaining days to the other parent. In other words, each parent is equally expected to share the childcare. Parents also have the right to cut back their work hours up to 25% until the child turns eight, with a commensurate reduction in pay. To help with the costs of child-rearing, the government also gives parents a monthly childcare payment until their children turn 16. All children are given free lunches at school until they turn 19. Children's health care, including dental care, is essentially free until the age of 20. And in some Swedish cities, including Stockholm, parents with infants and toddlers in prams (strollers) can ride for free on public buses, using large doors in the middle of the bus.

What impact have Sweden's policies had?[1,5] This is going to be a long list. Swedish fathers spend more time with their children and more time on housework than dads in the other 22 rich countries. They also spend less time at work, which leads to better physical and mental health. Swedish women are more likely to keep working after they have children since they don't have to shoulder so much of the childcare. Swedish couples also share the housework and childcare more equally. Regardless of whether they are married or not, Swedish parents are the most likely to stay together, raising their children in a two-parent home.[6]

Now here's where the Swedes really shine: When parents break up, custody laws automatically give both parents equal parenting time. The children will have two homes and live about equal time in each. And that's what most Swedish children do. Parents don't have to hire lawyers or go to court to fight over parenting time. Swedes assume that sharing the parenting time and responsibilities is just as important after the parents separate as it was when they lived together. Why should it be any other way? It's not only the kids who benefit, so do the parents. While children are living with their other parent, the child-free parent has more time to devote to work or education, to re-establish a social life, and to unwind and recharge from the demands of parenting. What kind of a wacky idea is this? As we will soon see, the science on this issue is consistently on the side of the Swedes.

This dumps a gnarly question right in our American laps: Why are our policies and laws so far behind? The go-to excuse is that paternity leaves and free daycare are far too expensive—a waste of taxpayers' money. Not so, according to scientists, including Nobel prize winning economist James Heckman, and Jane Waldfogel, a world authority on policies that affect the well-being of children and families. The costs of paternity leaves, free or subsidized childcare, and other family-friendly policies are far less than the expenditures taxpayers and employers incur with the current system. How can that be? Because taxpayer or employer money spent on these programs reduces the odds that these children will end up later in life costing taxpayers a ton of money due to dropping out of school, being incarcerated, having children at a young age without being married, paying less income tax because their salaries are so low, and relying on all kinds of welfare programs.[7,8]

Clearly, these kinds of policies are investments, and smart investors look for a reasonable return on their investments. Let's hone in on paid paternity leaves. Are they worth the considerable investment? And if they are, who benefits? A few representative studies echo what the larger body of research tells us.[7] When dads take leaves, both parents are less stressed, less physically exhausted, and less likely to become clinically depressed in the first year of their baby's life.[9] For example, in a study with 6,000 couples, when dads took paternity leave, the parents were 25% more likely to still be married five years later.[10] As for benefits to kids, in 1,300 lower income families, nine-year-olds had better relationships with their dad when he had taken a paternity leave when they were born.[11] A paternity leave can also be a matter of life or death, literally, for some babies. Children whose dads take paternity leaves are less likely to die during infancy.[7] This further highlights the ethical matter of fairness to children. Almost 75% of college educated workers versus only one-third of less educated workers are entitled to paid leaves after their child is born or adopted.[4]

What do our father myths have to do with any of this? A lot, as it turns out. Even in recent studies, many American fathers do not take a paternity leave even though their company offers it—and even though the typical leave is no more than two weeks.[12,13] These fathers say they are worried that if they take time off, their families will pay the price down the road. Though their employer might have an official leave policy, many men worry how their bosses or co-workers *really* feel about their taking a leave. Will the new dad get smaller raises, be passed over for promotions, or be left out of the loop for opportunities that eventually lead to more money? Dig deeper. Do you smell any aging, rotten father myths lurking about? Surely by now, you can smell these two stinkers: (1) The main contribution a dad can make to his children is his income and (2) babies don't need their dads as much as they need their moms. Is it hard to understand why many dads might feel they can't risk hurting their kids financially by taking a paternity leave?

Are dads who don't take paternity leaves just being paranoid? Unfortunately, they are not. Take what happened to Josh Levs, a CNN reporter and columnist, as described in his book, *All in: How Our Work First Culture Fails Dads, Families and Businesses*.[14] In 2012, Levs was working in Atlanta for Time Warner's CNN. When his third child was due and his wife was confined to bed for a time before the birth, Levs requested a ten-week leave. All female employees, including women who were surrogate mothers, were entitled to the leave. Fathers and mothers who adopted a child or who had a surrogate carry their biological child also got leaves. But a biological father, like Levs, whose wife was having their biological child was not entitled to a leave. Levs sued Time Warner. One year after his child was born, the company changed its policy. Since then, Levs has become a well-known spokesperson for policies such as paternity leaves and flex time schedules that allow fathers to be more fully engaged with their children.

Want more evidence that Americans are not "all in" on paternity leaves? Take a look at the story in Box 6.1 to see what happened to Pete Buttigieg, Secretary of Transportation, when he took a leave.[15,16]

Box 6.1 America's secretary of transportation mocked for taking paternity leave[15,16]

America's Secretary of Transportation, Pete Buttigieg, and his husband, Chasten, welcomed their adopted twins, Penelope and Joseph, into their family in August 2021. And Buttigieg took a four-week paternity leave to take care of their premature newborns. Then in October, on his nationally televised prime time show, Tucker Carlson, a Fox News host, mocked Buttigieg, saying he was on "paternity leave, they call it, trying to figure out how to breastfeed. No word on how that went." It's worth noting that Carlson's employer, Fox News, provides all male and female employees with a six-week paternity or maternity leave. Ironically, at that time, President Biden was advocating for legislation to create paternity and maternity leaves for all Americans. In response to Carlson's snide comments, Buttigieg told CNN's Jake Tapper, "I'm not going to apologize to Tucker Carlson or anyone else for taking care of my premature newborn infant twins. The work that we are doing is joyful, fulfilling, wonderful work."[17]

In short, America has a long way to go when it comes to workforce policies that encourage and support fathers' relationships with their children. Papas with prams (baby strollers) are a far bigger hit in other rich countries than in the U.S. And as we'll now see, America's child custody laws are not winning any prizes for father friendliness and gender equity or serving the best interests of the child.

CHILD CUSTODY LAWS

Since more than half of American parents split up well before their children turn 18, child custody laws have an enormous impact on millions of children. Keep in mind that custody laws also apply to children whose parents were never married. As things presently stand, almost 80% of these children end up living with their mother and spending varying amounts of time with their father. With dad having been largely demoted to an every-other-weekend "uncle," his relationship with his children generally becomes weaker and sometimes ends altogether. For reasons we discussed in an earlier chapter, many dads are swimming against the current to maintain their relationships with their kids—and one of the strongest currents in that stream is their state's custody laws.

Leaving aside how the parents feel, let's zero in first on what's best for the kids. Instead of guessing or arguing about this, let's take the rational approach: Rely on the research. By 2018, 60 studies had compared children's outcomes in two types of families.[18] The traditional option is the sole physical custody family where children live primarily or exclusively with mom and spend varying amounts of time with dad. The newer option is living with each parent at least 35% and usually 50% time year-round in a shared joint physical custody or shared parenting families. In the 60 studies, conducted in 15 countries over two decades, children ranged in age from infants to eighteen. The studies included well-educated, higher income parents, as well as less educated, less well-to do parents. The researchers looked at a wide range of outcomes, grouped into five general categories: grades and achievement tests; mental health (depression, anxiety); behavior (delinquency, aggression); physical health (including stress-related health problems); and children's relationships with their mothers, fathers, step-parents, and grandparents. In many studies, the researchers also considered how much conflict there was between the parents and factored that into the statistical analysis before comparing the children's outcomes.

The shared physical custody families won the contest. This held true even when the parents did not get along well, were not college-educated, and did not have high incomes. Did that make your head spin? Here's a head spinner: The parents did *not* have to be rich, well-educated, or cooperative buddies in order for their kids to benefit from living nearly equal time with each of them. In fact, when the parents did not get along well, their children usually had *better* outcomes when they lived with each parent nearly equally than when they lived only with their moms. Why? Because feeling close to dad and benefitting from what he had to offer by actually living with him (instead of seeing him every other weekend) offset a lot of the damage from their parents' bickering, backbiting, and badmouthing.[19]

Five states have taken the lead in custody law reform by placing children's relationships' with their fathers front and center—Arkansas, Arizona,

Kentucky, West Virginia, and Florida—certainly not the usual suspects for progressive policies. In these states, both parents are allotted at least 35% and up to 50% of the parenting time. It goes without saying that shared parenting laws do not apply when there is any history of domestic violence, child neglect or abuse, or problems such as drug or alcohol abuse or mental illness that would put the child in any danger while in a parent's care. Let's not get confused here. Even in these five states, parents are completely free to make their own plans. It's only if they cannot agree that their state's law comes into play.

Some states' laws are much more generous than others in giving children time with their fathers.[20] For example, in California, children spend an average of 120 days a year with their fathers—roughly a third of the parenting time. In contrast, in Tennessee, children spend an average of only 80 days a year with their fathers—a little over one-fifth of the parenting time. Are 40 days worth getting riled up about? Yes, they are. Why? Because custody plans remain in place from the time the parents separate, which might be when the child is only a few months old until the child turns 18.

Let's do some math to bring this closer to home. Assume you and your ex (whether you were married or not) separate when your child is three. You're the dad. You happen to live in a state where the custody laws typically award dads 20–25% of the parenting time. Over the next 15 years of your child's life, you will have *two years* less time together than you would have if you lived in a state where the standard was 33% time for each parent. And if you had lived in a 50/50 parenting law state, you would have *four and a half years* more time with your child. How would that make you feel as the parent—or as the adult child who has always wondered why your dad didn't spend more time with you after your parents split up?

But what do states' custody laws have to do with the father myths? Let's see if you can figure this out on your own. Ready? If most residents in your state believe the myths, they will vote for legislators who hold those same views. And who is in charge of making or revising the state's custody laws? The legislators. To further muddy the waters, within the same state, the gender role beliefs of judges, lawyers, and custody evaluators tend to be more liberal and less sexist in certain judicial districts than in others—with those living in the more metropolitan areas tending to be more progressive in regard to issues like shared physical custody. In many ways then, fathering time, so crucial to the well-being of children, is based on the luck of the draw.

Is there any reason to believe that judges or custody evaluators have any biases against dads? Yes, there is. Let's start with the judges. In these studies, researchers give judges and groups of citizens a hypothetical custody case and ask them how much parenting time they would award each parent. The contrast is startling. In studies from 2011 through 2021, most judges award the (hypothetical) dad far less parenting time than the mom—and far less time than the public would award him. The public is also more willing than judges to say the children should live half-time with each parent.[21–24] As for the power of fatherhood falsehoods, half of the judges in one 2006 study said children under the age of six should live with their mom because women have a "natural instinct" for mothering.[23] Similarly, in a 2021 study with 619 judges, those with more traditional, sexist gender role beliefs gave far less parenting time to the father than judges with less traditional, less sexist beliefs. The 500 citizens in the study gave more parenting time to the father than the conservative *or* the liberal judges gave him.[24] And in another 2021 study, 714 judges were more apt to favor the mother in allowing a parent to move farther away, taking the children with them. The move, of course, makes it difficult, if not impossible, for the other parent to spend nearly as much time with the kids as when the parents lived closer to each other.[25] The point is that many judges are out of sync with public opinion and are limiting children's time with their dads based on their false and sexist beliefs about fathers. Although judges have generally become more aware of how their racist biases affect their decisions, they seem to be far less aware of their sexist biases against fathers.

As for custody evaluators, things don't look much rosier in respect to sexism. Back in 2006, almost all custody evaluators in one study believed children under the age of five should never spend *any* overnight time with their fathers.[26] Unfortunately, more than a decade later, a group of expert child custody evaluators acknowledged that their profession was still sexist and biased against fathers. For example, evaluators often exaggerated the father's flaws and downplayed the mother's, which resulted in their recommending less fathering time. One example the researchers gave was a custody evaluator who considered the father drinking one beer every night to be a worse parenting problem than the mother having been arrested for drunk driving.[27] And one of the nation's leading experts on domestic violence has expressed grave concerns for decades about custody evaluators' biases against fathers based on their false beliefs about male and female violence.[28]

Are those legislators, judges, or custody evaluators who oppose shared or equal parenting for separated parents intentionally undermining children's relationships with their fathers? Of course not. Still, their unfounded beliefs about fathers end up depriving millions of children of the kind of fathering time that strengthens their bonds. In a sense then, child custody laws place a metaphorical "gate" between children and their fathers—a gate that, as we will now see, is largely under the control of the mother.

MOTHERS' POWER: THE GATEKEEPERS

Changing our custody laws and workforce policies will give fathers countless opportunities to counter the false beliefs that have held them back from being the fathers they want to be. Unfortunately, the process moves at a snail's pace. For example, in 2022, childcare legislation stalled again in Congress, largely due to Republican opposition, even though 60% of families who need childcare cannot afford it.[29] It also took years to revise the custody laws in the five states that eventually enacted shared parenting bills, while the other 22 states that are considering similar bills keep slogging along.[30]

Is there anything parents can do to take matters into their own hands? Yes, there is. Let's start with mothers. Mothers hold most of the power in deciding how involved the father will be allowed or encouraged to be with their child. Her behavior is rooted in her beliefs about fathers, beliefs that existed long before she ever became a mother. The mom has the power either to open or to close the metaphorical parenting "gate" between the father and their children—a situation known as gatekeeping.[31,32] Her beliefs and behavior either make it easier or make it harder for the dad to create a strong, loving bond with their child. Before we delve further into this, take the quiz in Box 6.2. The more of these behaviors the mother engages in, the more she is closing the parenting gate. How do the mothers in your family stack up?

Which mothers are the most likely to open the parenting gate?[32–35] Not surprisingly, mothers who refuse to buy into the fatherhood myths welcome their children's fathers through that gate. Gate-opening moms are more apt

Box 6.2 Gatekeeping quiz: How do mothers in your family stack up?[31]

Put an X by any of these behaviors that are part of your past or present. Think about the effect each behavior has on children.

Mother's Control Over Dad

__ Make him do what she wants him to do with the child
__ Monitor his time with the child
__ Impose her will on him
__ Keep him from making parenting decisions
__ Set the rules for how the parents
__ Supervise his interactions with the child

Encouragement by the Mother

__ Say positive things about how he talks and interacts with the child
__ Compliment him about his parenting
__ Ask his opinion about parenting
__ Say positive things like "you're good with the children"
__ Support him in completing a parenting task
__ Tell the child positive things about him

Discouragement

__ Tell other people what she dislikes about his parenting
__ Not cooperate with him on parenting tasks
__ Criticize him as a father
__ Roll her eyes at him when he talks or interacts with child to show her frustration
__ Tell the child what she thinks the father did wrong
__ Pretend to support his parenting decisions
__ Say sarcastic comments when he interacts with the child
__ Attempt to undermine his parenting decisions

to have grown up with loving, supportive dads in the home. And women who work outside the home are generally not as jealous or insecure about sharing the parenting since they derive their sense of identity and self-esteem from something in addition to raising children.

Let's take a closer look at a study of how jealousy affects gatekeeping.[36] In married families with a four-year-old child, wives criticized their husband more and did more to undermine his parenting when he was very involved in caregiving and nurturing than when he limited his interactions mainly to playing with their child. The mom didn't mind the dad being their child's playmate. But when he did stereotypical "mom" nurturing things, she felt jealous and insecure about herself as a parent—especially if the child was a girl. Let's replay that last part. Remember that one of the common fatherhood myths is that mothers are supposed to be much closer than fathers are to their daughters.[37] In this study, we see that myth taking hold even though the daughter is only four-years-old. A corollary to the jealous mom might be a jealous husband who feels bad about himself because his wife makes a lot more money than he does. He might criticize her more often or make snide remarks about her successes at work. It's okay if she "helps" earn part of the family income, but not okay if she completely outshines him.

Unfortunately, some mothers seem oblivious to the negative impact their gate-closing is having on their kids, as we can see from adult children's comments in Box 6.3. Not only is the gate-keeping mom damaging the kids' relationships with their dad, she is also shooting herself in the foot when her children are old enough to realize what's going on. Still, let's be careful not to demonize gate-closers. Most of these moms are not intentionally trying to lock the dad out of their children's lives. Many are unaware that their behavior and the false beliefs that guide it are having any negative impact on the kids. In fact, they probably acquired these false beliefs about fathers long before they became mothers. But that doesn't mean these mothers are villains who are purposely weaving some evil plot against dads. And, in case you're wondering, gay dads and lesbian moms also engage in gatekeeping. Still, in this study of adoptive parents, heterosexual mothers did the most gate-closing.[38]

Box 6.3 When mom closes the gate[39]

"Mom has always told me that women have a special intuition that men don't have. But I think what's really going on is that she'd be hurt if I was really close to dad."

"Mom tells me about their fights. This puts me in the middle. When they're fighting, she asks me to go to dinner with her. Once she actually turned the car around and drove us back home because I refused to listen to her complain about my dad."

"My mom doesn't have many friends. She has always told me and my sister about her arguments with dad. She's even asked us if we think she should leave him. It makes it very difficult to see him from my own perspective."

"If I talked to my dad about something personal, my mom would be really hurt. She'd feel replaced and her self-worth would be diminished."

"When dad and I are trying to talk, mom literally talks over him like he didn't exist. I can't get as close to him as I want because of her insecurity about not having a career."

As you'd expect, when parents separate, gatekeeping plays a much more powerful role in children's relationships with their dads.[40,41] Remember that custody laws generally give mothers almost all the parenting time. Even so, in every state, the mother has the legal power to give the father as much parenting time as she chooses. The parenting gate "hinges" on her feelings. Will she close the gate if she's really hurt or angry about the separation—or if she, her friends, or her lawyer are under the spell of the father myths? Will she close it whenever she gets really frustrated or mad at him? Will she threaten to close the gate as a way of emotionally blackmailing her ex into doing her bidding? In situations like these, can you hear the parenting gate slamming shut, hitting dad in the rear end as he retreats?

In its most extreme, toxic form, gate-closing can escalate into a situation known as parental alienation.[42,43] Parental alienation is an extremely damaging situation where one parent intentionally tries to turn the children against their other parent, weakening or entirely destroying their relationship. It is estimated that as many as 25% of children have experienced this. Even though the father can be the alienating parent, it is usually the mother. And although alienation can occur in married families, it's much more common after parents separate. In the most severe cases, children can become so alienated from their father that they refuse to have any contact with him, even years after their parents' separation.

Every mother has the power to reject the father myths and keep the parenting gate open, even if she is no longer living with the children's father. The dad may or may not walk through an open gate. The mom has no control over that. But it is her hands, not his, that controls the gate. Slam it shut. Open it wide. The choice is hers.

WHAT CAN FATHERS DO?

"A backbone is better than a wishbone." "God helps those who help themselves." "You can't prevent birds of sorrow and trouble from pooping on your head, but you can stop them from building a nest in your hair." So what can dads do on their own behalf?

As a basic blueprint for dads, let's consider what women have done to subvert sexist stereotypes about their group. They created national organizations and programs in schools and at work to raise awareness of sex discrimination. They marched angrily and publicly by the thousands, wearing "pussyhats" in 2017 to protest Donald Trump's crude comments about grabbing women by their genitals.[44] (In case you're wondering, no feminist ever burned her bra in any demonstration. At a relatively small protest against the 1968 Miss America contest, one of the 100 protesters took off her bra, eased it out from under her shirt, and tossed it into the "freedom trash can" along with items such as high heels, mops, and lipstick that symbolically representing getting rid of things that oppressed women.[45]) Women and their organizations brought about a more diverse and inclusive college curriculum, anti-discrimination laws, and nationwide awareness of discrimination, even in its most subtle forms. And these efforts continue to this day. Women also spread their messages with some slogans that can be pretty insulting to men: "A woman needs a man like a fish needs a bicycle."

Women even waged war against Teen Barbie dolls. Yes, for real, as you can see from Box 6.4.[46] And if that doesn't whet your appetite, sink your teeth into this story about McDonald's Happy Meals. In 2021, researchers wrote an article outing McDonald's for messages on their Happy Meals' boxes that some deemed insulting to girls—messages such as "girls try, boys aim high" that portray girls as less active, less powerful, and more in need of help than boys.[47] For sure, women's groups have not been timid or shy about going after the advertising industry for messages that insult or condescend to women or girls.

Box 6.4 Shut up, Teen Barbie[46]

In 1992, Mattel toy company released 350,000 Teen Talk Barbie dolls with a voice box that would speak when a button was pushed. One of the phrases was: "Math class is tough." Educators including the National Council of Teachers of Mathematics and the American Association of University Women lashed back, given the insulting sexist stereotypes about girls and math. The backlash was so fierce that Mattel offered to exchange the dolls for nonspeaking ones and deleted the math class phrase from future dolls. In 1993, adding more fuel to the fire, a group calling themselves the Barbie Liberation Organization secretly arranged to have the voice box of the G.I. Joe action figures installed inside the Teen Barbie dolls. These Barbies were found in stores in New York and California, speaking phrases such as: "Eat lead, Cobra!," "Attack!," and "Vengeance is mine!"

By comparison, fathers have been relatively reticent—and probably for a good reason. The public would not take kindly to throngs of angry men protesting against custody laws or paternity leave policies, let alone wearing tee-shirts with such slogans as: "A man needs a woman like a fish needs a bicycle." Still, millions of dads, especially younger ones, are not passively allowing themselves and their children to be bulldozed by these falsehoods. Dads have created their own fatherhood support groups and organizations, such as *City Dads*[48] and *Mr. Dad.*[49] Men and women are also working together in organizations like the *National Parenting Organization* to advocate for reform in child custody laws.[50] Some documentary filmmakers have also stepped up to educate the public about discrimination against fathers in child custody laws, for example, Ginger Gentile's documentary, *Erasing Family.*[51]

Stay-at-home dads have also organized the National At-home Dad Network, sharing advice and speaking out about their lives.[52] While their wives earn most or all of the family's money, these dads do the childcare and other work in the home. Despite all the talk about gender equity—for women at least—many of these men still get a lot of flak for being "unmanly," "losers," and "wimps" who either cannot or will not support their families. It feels very reminiscent of the insults once hurled at mothers who dared to work outside the home—being told they were "emasculating" (to put it politely) their husbands and that they shouldn't have had children in the first place if they weren't going to stay home to raise them. As a 2022 study of 94 newspaper and magazine articles about at-home dads tells us, Americans still have very mixed feelings about these fathers.[53] As we can see from the story in Box 6.5 about Shannon Carpenter, at-home dads take a lot of heat.[54] As Carpenter explains in his humorous yet serious advice book, for years, he has been the target of snide and insulting remarks, disapproving and suspicious looks, and hostile questions.

Box 6.5 Stay at home dads: Up close and personal[54]

What comes to mind when you hear the term stay at home dad? ... The term oozes with this vision of a dad without a manly bone in his body. It implies that his masculinity has been stripped and his balls have been replaced by fallopian tubes.

If you want to be passive aggressive, because it's fun, then maybe next time a nice summer Tuesday morning rolls around, you start sending them (people who criticize at-home dads) a shit ton of pics of you at the pool. Make sure you ask them how the traffic was on their drive to work that day. You can also remind them that the next time they have to work late again, they can take comfort in the fact that "eventually you will have time to see your kids, probably around high school."

At one point, I found myself sitting on the edge of the bathtub holding my daughter with her head over my shoulder as she went all Exorcist with projectile vomit, rocking my son in his car seat with my foot so he would stop screaming and watching my dog lick vomit off the baby.

You are not going to carry a diaper bag. You are going to carry an adventure bag. Think of yourself as more Indiana Jones and less Nanny McPhee.

Shannon Carpenter, *The Ultimate Stay-at-Home Dad: Your essential manual for being an awesome full-time father.*

THE PUBLISHING AND ENTERTAINMENT INDUSTRIES

Books, TV shows, and movies also need to pick up the pace to subvert father stereotypes with as much zest as they invested on behalf of women and girls. Parenting books should be more balanced and more forceful in calling out fatherhood falsehoods. For example, in a recent study of 23 child-rearing books, there were 3 times as many pictures of mothers as fathers. Mothers were almost always in charge of parenting, with fathers following directions as if they were inept sidekicks.[55] Books should emphasize and celebrate the father's importance no matter how old his children are, including grown-up kids.

Filmmakers also need to step up their game. There are still far too many movies that portray fathers at their worst. And because they are exceptions to the norm, certain movies stand out and receive nationwide attention. For example, the Academy Award nominated film, *King Richard,* received international attention for its portrayal of Richard Williams, the African American father of tennis superstars Serena and Venus Williams.[56] And the Netflix movie, *Fatherhood,* told the true story of a father who raised his daughter on his own after his wife died from an embolism shortly after giving birth.[57] Although the family whose story is told in the *Fatherhood* movie is white, casting the family as black further helped challenge racist and sexist stereotypes of black fathers. While these strides are commendable, the movie industry as a whole still has a long way to go in subverting father myths.

Television also continues to peddle plenty of demeaning stereotypes of dads. It's not surprising that this was the case ten years ago.[58] What's surprising is that these demeaning stereotypes are still so prevalent. For instance, in ten of the most popular sitcoms in 2017, dads came off looking far more incompetent, immature, and self-absorbed than moms. Working-class dads were made to look especially foolish, inept, and out of touch with their children—which taps into the myth that kids benefit most when dad makes plenty of money.[59]

Until recently, there were no shows about single fathers. In the eleven shows about single dads that existed in 2019, the dads were emotionally engaged with their kids. But most of them were either inept or overly dependent on outsiders to give them parenting advice.[60] Even in 2016, a group of ten scholars agreed that television still promotes too many negative messages about fathers.[61] Then too, in 34 top-rated family-oriented sitcoms, fathers were just as likely to be the butt of the joke in 2017 as they were in 1980. More troubling still, fathers in more recent sitcoms were *less* likely to engage in key parenting behaviors than they were in the earlier older sitcoms.[62] In short, TV sitcoms have a long way to go in promoting gender equity for fathers.

CHILDREN'S BOOKS AND TOYS: BENDING THE TWIG

"As the twig is bent, so grows the tree." What we teach children when they are young "twigs" has an impact on their future beliefs and choices in their lives. If we are sincere about not wanting fathers and mothers to be easily duped and manipulated by father myths, we need to "bend the twig" through the toys and books we give the very young children. Publishers and toy makers realized years ago that their products needed to be more diverse and inclusive—dolls that did not have white skin, books about single-parent or divorced families, science kits with pictures of girls on the package. The pictures and stories, even with animal characters, plant ideas in a young child's mind about what a family should or should not be. What do daddies do? What do mommies do? What is normal? What is weird?

To appreciate the power of books and toys, try this. Next time you have access to a children's storybook that has anything to do with a family or with parents, open it. First, just flip through and look at the pictures. Then go back and read the text. Even if the story is about a bunny rabbit family, what is the daddy doing? What is the mommy doing? Are there any father myths and stereotypes in the book?

Here's another experiment for you. Next time you're with parents who have a son under the age of four, ask them a few questions: "Have you ever given him a baby doll? If not, why not? Has he ever asked for a doll or ever shown any interest in dolls? How did you react? Does he have a stuffed animal—a bear, a dinosaur, a dog? Does he cuddle and talk to it and take care of it in a nurturing way? How do you feel about that? What's the difference in how you feel about the stuffed toy and a doll?" On that note, next time you're in a home where a very young girl lives, notice what kind of toys she has. Are there any "boy" toys? Why do her parents let her have "boy" toys if they won't let her brother have a doll?

Playing with a baby-type doll, unlike playing with an action figure or a more grown-up doll, teaches a young child how to be empathetic, tender, and nurturing. It also teaches them that this type of caretaking is not just for women and girls. There is nothing "feminine" about taking care of a baby—a pretend one or a real one. Still, many Americans are not on board with the idea of boys having a doll, as the comments in Box 6.6 remind us. In part, this is driven by the gender stereotype that baby work is women's work. And in part, it is driven by the fear that playing with dolls, dressing up in little girl costumes, or playing with "girl" toys will turn boys into "sissies"—a code word for gay or for males who have become so "femininized" that someday they will be "henpecked" wusses as husbands. The irony is that those same adults usually don't seem to mind if little girls play with "boy" toys or show very little interest in playing with dolls and other "girl" toys. Apparently, they are not worried that little girls will turn into lesbians or into women who are so masculine that men won't find them very desirable.

Box 6.6 Little boys with baby dolls: Yuck![63]

"My son had a doll when he was little. Carried it all over the place. He is a rough and tumble 12-year-old now who loves babies and will help babysit his cousins all the time. He was teased about the doll and I would put people in their place. Screw 'em all! Baby dolls don't do anything for boys except make them more caring."

"The Christmas before he got his baby sister, my all-boy rough & tumble, monster truck loving, camo wearing, hyper masculine nephew asked for a doll. He immediately named it Ben, put his baby boy clothes on it, and has been its 'Dad' ever since. He took care of Ben just like he saw his baby sister being cared for. Ben rides in his dump trucks, helps him do yard work, and they pretend to hunt together."

One toy company that stands out in showing us what could be possible is Hasbro. In 2019 Hasbro created a mind-blowing campaign for their "Baby Alive" dolls. The campaign showed touching scenes of little boys tenderly, comfortably, and earnestly taking care of their baby dolls under the slogan "we *all* can take care." The message, of course, was that caring for babies is not a feminine value or activity. It is a human value and activity. The other intent was to make parents address their own biases[64] In the even newer 2021 "Baby Alive" campaign, the slogan was "Ageless Care: Taking care lasts forever." These ads show boys and girls taking care of their dolls along with scenes of adult sons and daughters taking care of their elderly parents.[65] But here's the odd thing: Those ads were only released in Brazil even though Hasbro is an American company. What does that tell us? Ponder it.

Books, movies, and TV shows for children also need to back off the father myths. For example, in 200 of the best-selling children's storybooks, mothers are almost always in charge of childcare and are almost always shown as more nurturing than fathers.[66] Recent programs on Hulu specifically targeted at two- to four-year-olds are still gender stereotyped.[67] And in 61 Disney animated movies released between 1937 and 2019, there were *no* portrayals of dads as their children's caregivers.[68]

One of the most uplifting examples of how children's books and movies can subvert stereotypes is *Hair Love* written by Mathew Cherry. Cherry intentionally set out to defy the racist and sexist stereotypes about African American dads.[69,70] As an African American dad and former NFL player, Cherry decided to write a children's book. In the book, a black dad taking care of his daughter on his own while his wife is in the hospital. The dad struggles and eventually succeeds in styling his young daughter's hair—a touching and amusing journey that strengthens their bond. After the book became a bestseller, Cherry wrote and directed a film version which won the Academy Award for best animated short film in 2019. Cherry also advocates on behalf of the "Natural Hair Act," which allows African Americans to wear their hair in their natural styles at work or in school. As he told NBC News, "Black fathers get a bad rap in mainstream media, so I wanted to show them as present and caring, versus the deadbeat dad stereotype that is often ascribed to them in film."[70]

Children's books and certain toys have the power to "bend the twig" in ways that create a more father supportive "tree." And, as we will see, the advertising industry can also be a "twig-bender" when it decides to take an ax to the forest of anti-father "trees."

THE ADVERTISING INDUSTRY

Why did the United Kingdom pass a law prohibiting commercials from sending demeaning, sexist messages? This is not a "why did the chicken cross the road" joke. This is for real. In 2019 Britain created guidelines that prohibit commercials from reinforcing sexist stereotypes and derogatory messages about body image. For example, these ads would not pass muster: an ad showing children making a mess while dad props up his feet and mom vacuums, or an ad showing a man who can't change a diaper or a woman who can't park a car. And the British are not the only ones taking this leap. Other countries, including Belgium, France, Norway, South Africa, and India, have adopted similar advertising guidelines.[71]

In the U.S, women have made much more progress than men in pressuring the advertising industry to stop demeaning and stereotyping women or girls. Back in 2014, SHE media company even coined a term for this: femvertising. Femvertising means that companies' ads and marketing campaigns focus on women's issues, celebrate women, and seek to reduce gender stereotypes. SHE media also gives awards every year for ads that challenge gender norms and create positive views of women and girls. And researchers have jumped on board to find out if companies who win femvertising awards actually have policies and gender equity in their own companies.[72] The point is that there is no gender equity here because men do not have any type of "mascuvertising" movement or organization.

Still, in American advertisements, there are signs of progress on behalf of fathers. Take the most expensive, most talked about commercials of every year—the Super Bowl ads.[73] In 2015, the sentimental commercial, "With Dad," was voted the viewers' favorite and received more than 22 million views on YouTube. In 2016 Pantene hair products released their "Dad Do's" campaign, where NFL players tackled the tough job of styling their young daughter's hair.[74] The slogan was "Strong is beautiful: Girls who spend quality time with their dads grow up to be strong women." Then there are the ongoing "Dove Men Care" commercials first released at the 2014 Super Bowl—tear jerking, heartfelt scenes of real dads and their children.[75] Unilever corporation, maker of Dove products, really stepped up their game. In 2018 they launched a worldwide campaign to support paternity leaves, and in 2019 they enacted a policy giving three weeks paid paternity leaves for all employees.[75]

Now let's turn the advertising time machine back to 2012 when Clorox released an ad for bleach that read: "Like dogs or other house pets, new dads are filled with good intentions but lacking the judgment and fine motor skills to execute well." The online version of the ad included a lengthy description of "six mistakes new dads make" that was supposed to make us roar with laughter. The six mistakes included letting the baby eat stuff off the floor, putting its clothes on backward, not noticing food and play-dough smeared all over the baby's face, and trying to figure out why the baby, dressed in nothing but a onesie, is crying while dad is pushing it in a stroller outside on a cold, rainy day. Of course, these six mistakes would be inevitable since dads have the "skills and judgement" of a dog. There was enough backlash that Clorox removed the ad. Clorox would never dared to release such as ad comparing mothers to dogs: "Like dogs and other house pets, new moms are filled with good intentions but lack the judgement and fine motor skills to execute well."

To their credit, advertisers have made progress. Still, it is not hard to find print and social media ads and TV commercials that make dads look like buffoons and that perpetuate some of the worst stereotypes of men as parents. Keep in mind that children are the ones ultimately being harmed by these kinds of ads that mock and demean fathers.

Let's not misconstrue the message here. There's nothing wrong with movies, children's books, television shows, or commercials showing the worst or the most ridiculous aspects of any group of people. Poking fun at ourselves or at members of a particular group is fine, too, up to a point. The problem is a lack of balance in which groups repeatedly get portrayed as the bad guys and buffoons. The other problem is that certain topics are much more sensitive than others. For example, how about making some laugh-out-loud commercials about fat women or about mothers who don't work outside the home? How well would that fly? Thud. The "thud" test is a good one to use when watching "harmless fun" portrayals of dads.

MENTAL HEALTH WORKERS, DOCTORS, AND RESEARCHERS

Even if the advertising and entertainment industries are still shortchanging and stereotyping fathers, at least we can count on mental health professionals, social workers, doctors, and social science researchers to do right by dads and their children. Can't we? Actually, not so much. The greatest disservice many of these professionals are doing to fathers—and, therefore, to children—can be summed up in two words: ignore dad. Excluding and ignoring fathers play right into the hands of the master myth: Dads don't matter.

Let's focus first on doctors. The American Academy of Pediatrics has admitted that most pediatricians are ignoring fathers and should be doing more to include them in meetings or discussions about their children's health.[76] This is especially true for poor fathers living in inner cities whose children have chronic health problems.[77] A review of recent studies in epidemiology further confirms that health care providers are not paying enough attention to the importance of fathers in preventing and in treating physical and mental health problems of children of all ages.[78] Even though childhood obesity is a major health problem, in almost 667 studies of parents' roles in prevention or treatment, dads were almost completely excluded. While more than a third of the studies included only mothers, only 1% included only fathers.[79] Likewise, in studies on childhood autism, fathers are rarely included.[80]

Many social workers and mental health professionals also treat fathers as invisible and dispensable. In a national survey of child welfare workers, many believed fathers were unimportant, dangerous, and uninterested in their children. It made sense then not to involve the dads in any concerns about the welfare of their children in the mother's home.[81] As for the social science research, in the top five child development and family journals, from 1987 to 2000, there was only a small increase in articles about fathers.[82] In 200 academic papers about programs to improve parenting skills, the focus was almost exclusively on mothers.[83] As recently as 2018, fathers are still largely absent from the huge body of research on parenting.[84]

As for helping men and women work through problems that affect their parenting, fathers are once again left out in the cold to fend for themselves. For example, physicians at the University of North Carolina at Chapel Hill who had been caring for terminally ill mothers who died wanted to find support for their grieving husbands—men who were now left to raise their children on their own. There was no local or national program for widowers. So the doctors and the group of seven fathers had to form their own support group, which was eventually described in a best-selling book, *The Group: Seven Widowed Fathers Reimagine Life*.[85] In that same vein, in 29 studies about parents grieving the loss of their child during pregnancy, medical and mental health professionals had offered support for mothers but not for fathers.[86] The fact that new fathers are almost as likely as new mothers to become clinically depressed in the first year after their baby is born has gone largely unnoticed and untreated by mental health professionals.[87]

It's as if these professionals have hit the alt-delete button on fathers. They can delete him with a clear conscience because he didn't belong on the "parenting screen" to begin with. Out of sight, out of mind—the erased, invisible parent.

CONCLUSION: HELLO, HONEY! THE DADS ARE HOME

How do we know if we can succeed in subverting or eventually destroying the myths and stereotypes that demean, discourage, demonize, and disenfranchise dads?

Let's turn back the dial to 1955. What do we see? Only one in four mothers ever has a job outside the home. If a wife is too outspoken or too independent, her husband is mocked as a henpecked wuss who has lost his masculinity by letting his wife "wear the pants" in the family. Dads are pacing together (probably smoking) in hospital waiting rooms, never in the delivery room where their baby is being born. Paternity leave? What's that—a dad who leaves home without telling his wife where he's going?

Now reset the dial to 2023. Two out of three mothers work outside the home. Wives who are too timid or dependent are encouraged to stand up and speak up. Dads are expected to be part of the whole pregnancy process from the first ultrasound to the cutting of the umbilical cord. Paternity leave legislation is being discussed in Congress. Reset the dial again to 2050. Imagine. Just imagine.

Let's not fool ourselves. No matter how many workforce policies, custody laws, parenting books, movies, or commercials we change, and no matter how many mothers open the parenting gate, some men are still going to get an F as parents, as do some mothers. And that's that. But millions of other fathers are going to soar as parents when we remove the obstacles. As a society and in our own families, we need to do our level best to bury the myths and stereotypes that hold men back from giving their children, and the mother of their children, the best they have to offer.

REFERENCES

1. Glass J, Andersson M, Simon R. Parenthood and happiness: Effects of work-family reconciliation policies in 22 OECD countries. *Am J Sociol.* 2016;122:886–929.
2. Blomqvist P, Heimer M. Equal parenting when families break apart: Alternating residence in Sweden. *Soc Policy Adm.* 2016;50:787–804.
3. Staff. *Sweden: Early Childhood Education and Care.* European Commission; 2021.
4. Cohn J. I'm insanely jealous of Sweden's work-family policies. *New Repub.* June 22, 2014.
5. OECD. *Sweden's Support for Parents Is Comprehensive and Effective but Expensive.* Organization for Economic Cooperation and Development; 2021.
6. Altintas E, Sullivan O. Trends in father's contribution to housework and childcare under different welfare policy regimes. *Soc Polit.* 2017;24:81–108.
7. Waldfogel J. *Too Many Children Left behind: The U.S. Achievement Gap in Comparative Perspective.* Russell Sage Foundation; 2015.
8. Heckman J. *Invest in Early Childhood Development: Reduce Deficits, Strengthen the Economy.* University of Chicago; 2022.
9. Cardenas S, et al. Association between paid paternity leave and parental mental health across the transition to parenthood. *J Child Fam Stud.* 2021;44:online.
10. Carlson D, Knoester C. If I take leave, will you stay? Paternity leave and relationship stability. *J Soc Policy.* 2019;44:4–14.
11. Petts R, Knoester C, Waldfogel J. Fathers' paternity leave taking and children's perceptions of father-child relationships in the United States. *Sex Roles.* 2020;82: 173–188.
12. Harrington B, Fraone J, Lee J, Levey L. *The New Millennial Dad: Understanding the Paradox of Today's Fathers.* Boston College Center for Work & Family; 2016.
13. Bartel A. Paid family leave: Father's leave taking and leave sharing in dual earner households. *J Policy Anal Manage.* 2018;37:10–44.
14. Levs J. *All in: How Our Work First Culture Fails Dads, Families and Businesses.* Harper; 2015.
15. Rogers K. Pete Buttigieg joins the parental leave debate. *New York Times.* Published online October 18, 2021.
16. Thomas H. Tucker Carlson's insulting attack on Pete Buttigieg. *CNN news.* October 19, 2021.
17. Moniuszko S. Pete Buttigieg responds to Tucker Carlson mocking his paternity leave. *USA Today.* October 18, 2021.
18. Nielsen L. Joint versus sole physical custody: Outcomes for children in 60 studies independent of income and conflict. *J Child Custody.* 2018;15:35–54.

19. Nielsen L. Children's outcomes in shared versus sole physical custody: 60 studies considering income, conflict and quality of parent-child relationships. *J Divorce Remarriage*. 2018;59:237–281.

20. Hubin D. *State Custody Laws: 2019 Report Card*. National Parenting Organization; 2019.

21. Braver S, Ellman I, Votruba A, Fabricius W. Lay judgments about child custody after divorce. *Psychol Public Policy Law*. 2011;17:212–238.

22. Votruba A, Braver S, Ellman I, Fabricius W. Moral intuitions about fault, parenting and child custody after divorce. *Psychol Public Policy Law*. 2014;20:251–262.

23. Artis J. Judging the best interests of the child: Judges' accounts of the tender years doctrine. *Law Soc Rev*. 2006;38:769–806.

24. Miller A. Expertise fails to attenuate gendered biases in judicial decision making. *Soc Psychol Personal Sci*. 2019; 10(1):227–234.

25. Rachlinski J, Wistrich A. Benevolent sexism in judges. *Cornell Leg Stud*. 2021;58:101–142.

26. Ackerman M. *Clinicians' Guide to Child Custody Evaluations*. Wiley; 2006.

27. Klass J, Peros J. Ten signs of questionable practices in custody evaluations. *Am J Fam Law*. 2021;1:81–86.

28. Dutton D, Hamel H, Aaronson J. The gender paradigm in family court processes. *J Child Custody*. 2013;7:1–31.

29. Goldstein D. With child are scarce, states try to fix a broken market. *The New York Times*. June 18, 2022.

30. Chandler M. More than 20 states in 2017 considered laws to promote shared custody. *Washington Post, December 12*, 2017.

31. Puhlman D, Pasley K. The maternal gatekeeping scale. *Fam Relat*. 2017;66: 824–838.

32. Schoppe-Sullivan S, Altenburger L, Lee M, Bower DDC. Who are the gate-keepers? Predictors of maternal gatekeeping. *Parent Sci Pract*. 2015;15:166–186.

33. Ganong L, Coleman M, Markham M. Predicting postdivorce coparental communication. *J Divorce Remarriage*. 2011;52:1–18.

34. Cannon E. Parent characteristics and antecedents of gatekeeping. *Fam Process*. 2008;47:501–519.

35. Gaunt R, Pinho M. Do sexist mothers change more diapers? Ambivalent sexism, maternal gatekeeping and the division of childcare. *Sex Roles*. 2018;79:176–189.

36. Jia R, Schopppe-Sullivan S. Relations between coparenting and father involvement in families with preschool-age children. *Dev Psychol*. 2011;47:106–118.

37. Nielsen L. *Father-Daughter Relationships: Contemporary Research and Issues*. Routledge, second edition; 2019.

38. Sweeney K, Goldberg A, Garcia R. Not a mom thing: Predictors of gatekeeping in same sex and heterosexual parent families. *J Fam Psychol*. 2017;31:521–531.

39. Nielsen L. *Improving Father-Daughter Relationships: A Guide for Women and Their Dads*. Routledge; 2020.

40. Austin W, Fieldstone L, Pruett M. Bench book for assessing parental gatekeeping in parenting disputes. *J Child Custody*. 2013;10:1–16.

41. Ganong L, Coleman M, Chapman A. Gatekeeping after separation and divorce. In: Drozd L, Saini M, Olesen N, eds. *Parenting Plan Evaluations: Applied Research for the Family Court*. Oxford University Press; 2016:308–346.

42. Harman J, Warshak R, Lorandos D, Florian M. Developmental psychology and the scientific status of parental alienation. *Dev Psychol.* 2022;44:1–15.
43. Warshak R. *Divorce Poison: How to Protect Your Family from Bad-Mouthing and Brain-washing.* Regan Books; 2010.
44. Garfield L, Robinson M. Thousands of women wore pink pussy hats the day after Trump's inauguration. *Business Insider online.* January 21, 2017.
45. BBC. 100 women: The truth behind the bra-burning feminists. *BBC news online.* September 7, 2018.
46. Firestone D. While Barbie talks, G.I. Joe goes shopping. *The New York Times.* December 31, 1993.
47. Hourigan K. Girls try, boys aim high: Language on McDonald's happy meal boxes. *Sex Roles.* 2021;84:377–391.
48. City Dads. *City Dads Group. Com.*; 2022.
49. Matlock T. http://thegoodmenproject.com; 2009–Present.
50. National Parenting Organization. *National Parenting Organization.* www.national-parentsorganization.org; 2015.
51. Gentile G. *Erasing Family.* Gentile Film Productions; 2019.
52. Staff. The national at-home dad network. athomedad.org; 2022.
53. Kuperberg A, Stone P, Torie L. He's Mr. Mom: Cultural ambivalence in print news depictions of stay at home fathers, 1987–2016. *Gend Soc.* 2022;36:313–341.
54. Carpenter S. *The Ultimate Stay at Home Dad.* Penguin Life; 2021.
55. Fleming L, Tobin D. Popular child-rearing books: Where is daddy? *Psychol Men Masculinity.* 2005;5:18–24.
56. Andrews H. "King Richard" serves up something seldom seen. *Washington Post online.* November 20, 2021.
57. Tinubu A. In Netflix's "Fatherhood" Kevin Hart gives a white dad's memoir new layers of meaning. *NBC News Think online.* June 17, 2021.
58. Kelly J. Fathers and the media: Introduction to the special issue. *Fathering.* 2009;7:107–113.
59. Troilo J. Stay tuned: Portrayals of fatherhood to come. *Pop Media Cult.* 2017;6:82–94.
60. Turchi J, Bernabo L. Mr. Mom no more: Single father representations on television. *Crit Stud Media Commun.* 2020;42:437–450.
61. Podnieks E. *Pops in Pop Culture: Fatherhood, Masculinity and the New Man.* Palgrave MacMillan; 2016.
62. Scharrer E. Disparaged dads? A content analysis of depiction of fathers in U.S. sitcoms over time. *Psychol Pop Media.* 2020;44:4–5.
63. Samuels, R. Boys playing with dolls: City Dads.org; 2021.
64. Burns W. Hasbro appeals to parents: Boys can play with dolls. *Forbes.* Published online April 29, 2019.
65. Adeolu M. Hasbro's new Baby Alive campaign positions dolls as elder care learning tools. *Mark News Strategy.* Published online September 28, 2021.
66. Quinn S. Depictions of fathers and children in best-selling picture books. *Fathering.* 2009;7:140–158.
67. Kang S, Hust S. Traditionally and narrowly defined: Gender portrayals in television programming targeting babies and toddlers. *Sex Roles.* 2022;86:576–586.

68. Shawcroft J. Depictions of gender across eight decades of Disney animated film. *Sex Roles.* 2022;86:346–365.

69. Cherry M, Harrison V. *Hair Love.* Kokila; 2019.

70. Aviles G. "Hair Love" wins Oscar for best animated short film. *NBC News.* February 8, 2020.

71. Siegel R. Women who can't park cars, men who can't change diapers. Britain bans ads depicting harmful gender stereotypes. *Wash Post June 17.* Published online 2019.

72. Sterbenk Y. Is femvertising the new greenwashing? *J Bus Ethics.* 2022;177:491–505.

73. LaMonica P. These Super Bowl ads made this dad cry. *CNN Bus.* 2015;February 1, 2015.

74. Bowerman M. NFL dads do their daughter's hair in sweet Pantene ad. *USA Today.* February 4, 2016.

75. Unilever Staff. *Dove Men Paternity Leave for All Dads.* Unilever Corporation; 2019.

76. Allport B, et al. Promoting father involvement for child and family health. *Acad Pediatr.* 2018;18:746–753.

77. Kobylianski A. Experiences of inner city fathers of children with chronic illness. *Clin Pediatr (Phila).* 2018;57:792–801.

78. Yogman M, Garfield C. Fathers' roles in the care and development of their children: The role of pediatricians. *Pediatrics.* 2016;138:115–125.

79. Davison K. Fathers' representation in observational studies on parenting and child-hood obesity: A systematic review. *Am J Public Health.* 2016;106:14–21.

80. Rankin J, Paisley C, Tomeny T, Eldred S. Fathers of youth with autism spectrum disorders: A systematic review of the impact of fathers. *Clin Child Fam Psychol Rev.* 2019;55:1–20.

81. Bellamy J. A national study of male involvement among families in contact with the child welfare system. *Child Maltreat.* 2009;14:255–262.

82. Goldberg W, Tan E, Thorsen K. Trends in academic attention to fathers. *Fathering.* 2009;14:159–179.

83. Panter-Brick C, et al. Engaging fathers: Recommendations for game change in parenting based on a systematic review of global evidence. *Child Psychol Psychiatry.* 2014;55:1187–1212.

84. Cabrera N, Volling B, Barr R. Fathers are parents, too! Widening the lens on parenting for children's development. *Child Dev Perspect.* 2018;12:152–157.

85. Rosenstein D, Yopp J. *The Group: Seven Widowed Fathers Reimagine Life.* Oxford University Press; 2018.

86. Due C, Chiarollli S, Riggs D. The impact of pregnancy loss on men's health and wellbeing: A systematic review. *BMC Pregnancy Childbirth.* 2017;17:315–329.

87. Gross C, Marcussen K. Postpartum depression in mothers and fathers. *Sex Roles.* 2017;76:290–305.

INDEX

Note: Page references in **bold** denote tables.

relationships with dads 35;
remarriage after divorce 90; single
26, 65; and stereotypes 2–3, 6, 106,
117, 123; Swedish 107; in time-
consuming jobs 63; *see also* divorced
mothers; maternal instinct;
mothering skills
Woods, Tiger 86

work and family 73
workplace and childcare policies
106–109

*You Just Don't Understand: Men
and Women in Conversation*
(Tannen) 74
YouTube 123

Milton Keynes UK
Ingram Content Group UK Ltd.
UKHW020721230524
443010UK00013B/126